WHY ADVERTISING FAILS

Published by Advantage, Charleston, South Carolina.
Member of Advantage Media Group.

ADVANTAGE is a registered trademark, and the Advantage colophon is a trademark of Advantage Media Group, Inc.

Printed in the United States of America.

10 9 8 7 6 5 4 3 2 1

ISBN: 978-1-64225-346-7
LCCN: 2021916418

Cover design by David Taylor.
Layout design by Wesley Strickland.

This publication is designed to provide accurate and authoritative information in regard to the subject matter covered. It is sold with the understanding that the publisher is not engaged in rendering legal, accounting, or other professional services. If legal advice or other expert assistance is required, the services of a competent professional person should be sought.

Advantage Media Group is proud to be a part of the Tree Neutral® program. Tree Neutral offsets the number of trees consumed in the production and printing of this book by taking proactive steps such as planting trees in direct proportion to the number of trees used to print books. To learn more about Tree Neutral, please visit www.treeneutral.com.

Advantage Media Group is a publisher of business, self-improvement, and professional development books and online learning. We help entrepreneurs, business leaders, and professionals share their Stories, Passion, and Knowledge to help others Learn & Grow. Do you have a manuscript or book idea that you would like us to consider for publishing? Please visit advantagefamily.com.

Never Again Be An Advertising Victim, Discover The Secrets To Creating A <u>Successful Advertising and Marketing System</u> For Your Business, Products and Services...

Get _THE_ System That Business Owners Just Like You Have Used To Radically Transform Their Advertising From Ineffective and Wasteful Into A Business Asset That Will <u>Predictably and Reliably Deliver A Steady Stream Of New Customers, Clients, Patients and</u> _<u>Profits to the Bottom Line!</u>_

In This Master Class, You'll Discover:

☾ The difference between **Lead Generation** and **Brand Building**, and why lead generation almost always **TRUMPS** the latter.

☾ In most cases, THIS one form of advertising is only **wasting your time and money** for **<u>minimal results.</u>**

☾ THIS form of advertising will have you **<u>seeing returns in days, weeks, or months</u>** instead of wondering what the expense brought to you in return a year down the road.

☾ How YOU can be successful **<u>without</u> having to worry about how many people know your brand by name.**

☾ Learn how advertising in certain media outlets that have **<u>nothing</u>** to do with your business can actually make **A LOT** of sense and be **<u>very beneficial.</u>**

☾ How to **<u>model</u>** the marketing strategies of national companies in a way that will **translate their success into a <u>local level.</u>**

4 Amazing Bonus Gifts Valued at $938.97

Bonus Gift 1:
FREE Lead Generation Advertising Mastery Video Master Class
$297.00 Value

Bonus Gift 2:
The Best Of Dan Kennedy Collection
$497.97 Value

Bonus Gift 3:
Dan Kennedy's 10 Rules Of Direct Response Advertising Check List
$47.00 Value

Bonus Gift 4:
30 Day _FREE Trial_ of the 'Famous' No B.S. Marketing Newsletter and Magnetic Marketing Gold Membership
$97.00 Value

Request Instant FREE Access At www.WhyAdvertisingFails.com/Gift

Contents

Author's Important Introduction

MOST ADVERTISING FAILS. It is often not the fault of the advertising, per se, but rather of unrealistic expectations or of misuse. This is often not the fault of the small business owner either; he believed the correct thing for him to do was to become an expert of the "doing" in his business—dentistry, law, home remodeling, running a restaurant, etc.—not an expert in advertising. Unfortunately this leaves that business owner very, very vulnerable. I call them "advertising victims."

So, *most* advertising fails to achieve what its owner and payer hoped for—even to the extent of defying accurate accountability so the owner can't even say for certain what, if anything, it is doing.

In this book, we'll explore the different reasons for your advertising disappointing you more often than not, in blunt and straightforward terms. This may be uncomfortable and challenging but may also be enlightening and empowering.

Now, why listen to me about this?

First, I have no hidden agenda. I retired from ad copywriting as one of the highest-paid freelancers in America, routinely earning six-figure fees and royalties per project, year after year, with over 80 percent of clients using me repeatedly. This book is *not* a disguised sales letter for my services. The organization distributing it, originally founded by me—No BS Inner Circle/Magnetic Marketing—would love to have you as a Member, but bluntly, it doesn't matter to me one way or the other what you decide about that. And there are ways to test those waters entirely free of cost or obligation. So, relax about disguised agendas—there aren't any.

> **I have helped countless small business owners take these matters into their own hands and *successfully* use their advertising to build big, even really, really big businesses, all the way to billion-dollar revenues.**

Second, I bring a lifetime of relevant experience to this discussion. I grew up with the advertising business as a kid and have stayed in it my entire adult life. I have witnessed firsthand the insanity and corruption of the ad/media agency industry and how it takes advantage of its advertising victims. I have helped countless small business owners take these matters into their own hands and *successfully* use their advertising to build big, even really, really big businesses, all the way to billion-dollar revenues. My invented Magnetic Marketing® became a *movement*, literally changing the way advertising is done by leaders of over two hundred different business niches and categories and professions, here and abroad. You'll hear more about that in chapter 4. In total, I have profoundly influenced over one million business owners annually, and directly, personally altered the advertising approaches of thousands of businesses. From all that comes this book.

Third, I have always eaten my own cooking. I have used the exact same methods prescribed in this book and provided them to clients to start, grow, and grow rich with businesses and products of my own. I am not an academic theorist or an "empty expert."

Last, the reasons to listen to me about this will evidence themselves throughout this book, by your own good judgment. **You will find me presenting truths you have long suspected, but you felt alone in your suspicions, so you may have kept silent and, worse, gone along to get along—invested *your* money in advertising you felt was of little merit or productivity.**

Be More Skeptical

There is almost nothing I agree with Bill Maher about politically, but I agree wholeheartedly with his urging people to *"be more skeptical."* If you have doubts about your industry's norms, your peers' business practices, your industry's experts' advice, as the late, great industrialist Jack Welch advised: trust your gut. If it seems to you that "there's something wrong with this," go ahead and question it, hard. Your doubts about what you have been told to do with your advertising may be what motivated you to read this book. That discomfort and skepticism, that voice in your head telling you *"This* can't be right" and "There *must* be a better way" is very likely on to something!

Not to insult, but Barnum once put a dozen shills on a busy sidewalk, all carrying umbrellas and often stopping to look up at the cloudless, sunny sky. Within an hour, a little stand set up selling umbrellas was doing a booming business. This book is intended to stop such behavior, at least with your advertising buys!

The Mouse That Ill-Advisedly Roared

THIS WILL LIKELY be the chapter you like the least and find most irritating, so we might as well get it out of the way at the start. I'm told pearls are produced by irritating oysters. I have a long-, longtime client that I started with when it was tiny and stayed to around $1 billion. Its cofounder said that the entire time he could count on me to be *annoying*. He cited that as part of my value—that I would point out the ugliest elephant in a room everyone else was studiously ignoring. So, I will briefly, deliberately be annoying here in chapter 1. After that, I'll be more genteel. I promise. Really.

> If you "roar" and attract lots of attention but can't back up all the noise you make, you will wind up some lion's dinner.

No advertising, no matter how clever or slick, no matter its quantity, can long overcome a product or experience that is disappointing or frustrating for the customer, client, or patient. If you "roar" and attract lots of attention but can't back up all the noise you make, you will wind up some lion's dinner. It happens all the time: somebody with a good business idea and with good advertising, but the inability or unwillingness to follow through on it with consistent satisfying of customers, awakens a sleeping competitor, a bigger but less imaginative entity, or another entrepreneur willing to do a start-up, and that awakened "lion" roars louder than the mouse and backs it up. If you "roar" and attract a lot of customers who do not stick with you, because their experience with you fails to match their expectations created by your advertising, the costs of new customer acquisition coupled with poor retention eat you alive. "Churn" of customers that are of low value because of infrequent purchasing, leaving altogether after short tenure, and (some percentage) not ascending to higher levels of premium price activity is, almost without exception, unsustainable. It is a rotting, termite-infested, weak, and weakening foundation. There may be a shiny, gleaming Taj Mahal built atop it, there may be a lot of top-line gross, but inevitably, the entire structure is going to crash.

When Domino's Pizza went from little mouse to lion on the strength of its original, then-unique promise—*Fresh, Hot Pizza Delivered in 30 Minutes or Less*—it had to be certain it could actually do that. When it became impossible to back up the promise, in very different geographic areas, with size, with rising legal liability attached to drivers, etc., they had to pivot to an entirely different approach. I am a fan of writing the greatest ad first, then building the product or service to fulfill it—but when that can't or won't occur, it has to be "back to the drawing board."

As a lifetime "ad man," I frankly find it maddening to so often see and experience this dichotomy, with the advertising shouldering the blame for actually being too good for the product, services, staff, or consumer experience being advertised. To win big, the advertising must *be able to* make big, bold, exciting, reassuring promises and have the customer experience fulfill or even outperform them, every single time.

You have to be "ready and able." It does no good to make the phone ring with advertising but have it take twenty rings before it is answered, or let your front desk staff go to lunch together—routing calls during prime time to Battleaxe Bertha in Accounting, or to voice mail. It does no good to bring people through the doors with advertising if their first experience is "here, fill out these forms" or an unclean environment or obvious and anxiety-inducing chaos. It does no good to rack up first transaction sales with customers who then get no significant and impressive "welcome to the family" follow-up, no organized effort to bring them back. It does no good to get customers with advertising but pour them into a bucket with more leaks than bucket. And this is not just a matter of figuring out and defining "best practices" for every little detail in your business—it also requires diligent monitoring and determined enforcement. About this, in depth, see my book *No B.S. Ruthless Management of People and Profits*.

There should be no need to belabor this point, so I won't. The challenge to you is twofold: first, *never assume* the customer experience is meeting or, preferably, exceeding the expectations created by your advertising. Be ever vigilant. *Do* sweat even the small stuff. Take *extreme* pains *not* to be a roaring mouse. Second, develop the biggest, boldest, most attractive, most compelling advertising messages for your business that you can, and then "stretch" to live up to them.

CHAPTER 2:

The Blind Following the Blind

THEY'VE GOT A talking lizard. We'll get an emu with a goofy hat and sunglasses. Makes you think you might need a cow on roller skates singing opera. But what if They are playing an entirely different financial game than you are? Worse, what if They have no honest measurement of what, if anything, their "cute" advertising is accomplishing? *What if you are watching a parade of fools*—a parade you don't want to join? But how could *that* be?

To remind me of reality, I have a big button with a picture of the lion from Disney's *The Lion King*. When I push it, in his voice, it says: "I am surrounded by idiots." I know it is

> The environs of corporate America are loaded up with people in leadership and decision-making positions who have no idea what they are doing!

hard to believe, but the environs of corporate America are loaded up with people in leadership and decision-making positions who have no idea what they are doing!

There is *a dangerous tendency* to believe that the decision makers spending fortunes on their advertising *must* know more than you do. Jake Steinfeld, famous fitness guru and brilliant direct marketer, wrote a book provocatively titled *I've Seen a Lot of People Naked and They've Got Nothing on You*, about the dangerous tendency to credit others with being somehow inherently superior. Well, I've seen a lot of big spenders on advertising and corporate CEOs "naked," and I can promise you, they've got nothing on you. In fact, after you study just the next chapter, you will know more about *properly purposed* advertising than most big business CEOs, most holders of college degrees in business, and virtually all small business owners, including your competitors.

In the next chapter we'll get very granular and deal with the different types of advertising to be used for different purposes. But first, here I have to try to persuade you that virtually *all* of what you see done with advertising in your niche or business category does *not* represent "wisdom."

You can't afford to be led by what you see a majority doing. In personal behaviors, the majority of people engage in all sorts of obviously unhealthy, unconstructive, ill-advised behaviors. You know this. It follows that what you see the majority of companies and business owners doing is unlikely to be the wisest behavior. **It takes creativity and courage to act against common norms, so those norms are reinforced by most—after all, the majority are neither creative nor courageous. Specific to advertising, you dare not be led by the common, most widely acted out norms.** At best, doing so plays to getting "normal" (i.e., "average") results and risks being lost in a morass of close copycats. But you want extraordinary results, requiring you to stand out and stand apart from the crowd.

A mortal hazard is the peer and industry or profession pressure to conform to "*the* way *it* is done" in *your* business or profession. The tendency is to think this is based on a standard of success, but truth is that it is mostly merely "monkey see, monkey do." And with it failing, nobody wants to admit it, so it is continued by "see no evil, speak no evil." Of course if this were our approach to everything, as Mike Vance[1] often said, we'd still be lighting our homes and offices with gigantic candles and commuting to work with very big pooper scoopers. Actually, a lot of success with advertising for a particular kind of product or service comes from *defying* "the way it is done."

Here's a prime example: pillows. Pillow manufacturers mostly advertise to the trade, to persuade mattress, furniture, and home goods retailers to stock and sell their products. *That's* the *way* it *is done.* The owner of the pillow manufacturing company does not blanket the TV with commercials he stars in, selling his pillows direct to consumers, promising "the best night's sleep of your entire life— guaranteed." That is *not* how *it* is supposed to be done. *Unless* you'd like to bypass all distribution channel barriers and gatekeepers and get very, very rich advertising and selling pillows.

---

1   Mike Vance was, for a time, the dean of Disney University, worked with Walt on the development of Epcot, and later had a stellar career as a creative thinking teacher, a consultant to leading corporations like Marriott, and an author of a number of great books, including *Think Outside the Box.* I brought Mike in on several occasions to speak to my groups. His longtime associate, Diane Deacon, continues their work and can be found at www.creativethinkingassoc.com.

CHAPTER 3:

The Secret of *Properly Purposed* Advertising

I NEVER WANT you to advertise *just to advertise* again!

You have a toolbox at home somewhere. There's probably a flashlight in it, a hammer in it. If you blow a fuse, the flashlight can be a very useful tool in the dark basement closet containing the fuse box. The hammer, however, is not a good way to get the fuse back on. If you need to pound in a nail, the flashlight is a poor tool for that job, but the hammer is ideal.

Advertising works the same way, which is why **blindly copying others' advertising is so dangerous and foolhardy**; they may have a different chief purpose than you do, and they *may* have selected the right advertising tool for *their* purpose, but if you don't share their purpose, their tool is the wrong tool for you.

As an example, consider big, publicly traded companies versus privately owned small businesses. The big company traded on the please and puff up the feathers of the client. The more any type of agency talks to you about your image and brand awareness, the more you should worry. The prettier and fancier they want to dress up your advertising, the more skeptical you should be. If you are going to pour your money into this type of advertising, you should have a very good, rational reason for doing so and understand the patient capital required.

2. ONE-STEP/BUY NOW

This is what you see *most* retailers and professional practices doing, from car dealers to chiropractors, from furniture stores to financial advisors: some version of "come on in"—for the sale of the century or the free exam or the free tax planning seminar or one-on-one appointment. Again, do *not* be gulled by the fact that this is what you see the most of. That does *not* make it smart. It only makes it common.

This type of advertising, with rare exception, can only attract the relatively small percentage of its reached audience who are ready to buy now and are shopping with that in mind. But it offers nothing—no path for the much larger audience that notices the advertising, is made curious by it, but is nowhere near ready to buy, so they never make themselves known to the advertiser. By basically disinviting these people, you take your ad dollar and reduce it to twenty cents or less before it even gets out the door to go to work on your behalf. If you are going to do that, at least be very much aware of what you are doing.

An alternative to this is advertising that offers **multiple *reasons* to respond** as well as multiple *means* of responding, so that you get the ready-to-buy-now customer, but you also, *additionally* get others (*more!*) who are ready (only) to be nurtured, made to trust, and brought to being ready to buy. This is a more sophisticated approach, requiring more thought and know-how and systemization, but *you can do it*, and you can make your every ad dollar worth a lot more by doing so.

Or another alternative to Buy Now is full replacement of it with pure lead generation advertising, which we'll get to in a few minutes. First, let me give you a couple of examples of the *multiple reasons/ multiple means* approach:

For a financial advisor

PS: If you can't attend our important and timely tax law changes seminar, at least let me send you my new, "hot off the presses" *free report: 7 New Tax Traps Affecting Your Retirement Savings & Income*. No cost, no obligation. Just call 000-000-0000 or go to TaxTrapsReport.com.

Or if you're just unsure about attending the seminar, watch a ten-minute *free preview video* at SeminarPreview.com.

For a furniture store

PS: If you're not ready to come in and shop this weekend, at least us send you our new, illustrated book *25 Room Transformations for Less Than $99 a Month*. Just call 000-000-0000 and ask for it or visit AmazingNewRooms.com. While you're there, watch a *free video* featuring three home makeovers and enter our contest to win a complete new living room!

Most business owners accustomed to doing One-Step, One Reason to Respond Advertising *fear* that this tactic will downgrade Buy Now customers to delayed buyers, possibly lost with the lapsed time. They also aren't organized to manage leads with a complete marketing system. If that is corrected, as described in chapter 4, the fear is invalid 90 percent of the time; more is gained than is lost by principally continuing to advertise for your Buy Now customers but *also* inviting those not there yet to "at least" engage in a different, less threatening way than by "coming in."

Just as an example, in a split test I ran with a major healthcare chain of over one thousand offices, the ad with multiple reasons and multiple ways to respond did, in fact, reduce the number of instant free exam appointments by about 10 percent, but it produced about 30 percent additional leads requesting and getting a "free information kit." More than half of those converted to free exam acceptance, and the closing rate was better with those taking the delayed sale path than going in one leap to free exam. In net dollars this change to the ad yielded about $15,000 more per location, per month. (If you aren't sure if you could use an extra $15,000 a month, go ask your spouse.)

A similar strategy used with a financial advisor produced a year-to-year increase of more than $5 million in annuity and other financial product sales directly from *non*-Buy-Now leads obtained from the same ads and ad budget used to fill free seminars every month. Don't miss the important point here: the *same* ads with the slight tweak to multiple reasons to respond and the *same* ad spend filled two buckets instead of just one.

However, if you are emotionally and irrationally married to simple One-Step, Buy Now Advertising, or you refuse to put a robust follow-up system in place to nurture and ultimately convert leads, then at least keep this front and center in your mind: the offer in the "come in this week" call to action must be as "rich" and irresistible as you can make it. Ordinary, plain vanilla offers won't cut it.

3. LEAD GENERATION ADVERTISING/ MULTISTEP FOLLOW-UP

This type of advertising makes *no* **attempt at** instantly driving potential customers, clients, or patients to an appointment, a "consultative" call, a free estimate for work to be done, a "come on in now" of *any* kind. Instead, it is *entirely* **focused on** lead generation, by a free offer, most often of relevant information. I coined the term "info-first" for this type of advertising.

This is *not* simply "call for free brochure." The media offered must feature relevant *information*. There is stated or implied benefit, whether the respondent does anything beyond getting the information or not. It is titled and described to impute value just as if it bore a price rather than being free.

This type of advertising is sometimes branded but sometimes unbranded.

A good example of branded, as I write this, is Fisher Investments. Their TV, radio, and print ads identify the advertiser, Fisher Investments, but there is *no* attempt to move you to a phone or in-person appointment with a sales representative, to a free seminar, even to an online event; the ads are pure lead generation purposed, focused on Info-First, offering free guides, reports, and "bonus" reports titled and aimed at the soon-to-retire or retired person with assets exceeding $500,000. In financial services, Fisher is, by far, the biggest lead generation advertiser. They know what they are doing— but not just with the advertising, but with lead management and development.

Unbranded Info-First Advertising focused on pure lead generation can often generate more leads, thus achieving a lower cost per lead, by not getting a brand identity and preconceived notions about it in the way of the response. An example of an unbranded financial ad is:

This is a photo of me in my 1986 Rolls-Royce convertible formerly owned by Dean Martin. It is an excellent "tool" for a pleasant drive on a sunny day, but it is a poor "tool" for plowing a field or for moving freight. Choose your advertising tools wisely!

CHAPTER 4:

Advertising *Doesn't* Live on an Island

ONE OF THE great "dumb" shows I grew up with was *Gilligan's Island*. The silly premise was a small group out on a three-hour tour was grabbed by the sea and deposited on a distant island. The castaways were exaggerated types: the girl next door; the sexy super-model; the professor—ostensibly, the smart one; the super-rich, out-of-touch couple; the amiable buffoon, the captain; and, of course, Gilligan, essentially a Jerry Lewis type. I don't know if this influenced Larry David or Jerry Seinfeld, but in many ways *Seinfeld* was *Gilligan's Island* on a tiny square on the island of Manhattan, both shows "about nothing." In many respects, many if not most people live "small," as if on islands. This became magnified by COVID-19 and its "locked down" ramifications. Isolation, however, tends not to work well for most people. We are hardwired as social creatures, who need to be part of a "system" of living, and if deprived of one,

One of the main reasons advertising fails is that it is separated and isolated rather than part of a start-to-finish *system*.

if possible, we create one, as the castaways did for themselves on *Gilligan's Island*.

Advertising fares even worse in isolation than does a person.

One of the main reasons advertising fails is that it is separated and isolated rather than part of a start-to-finish *system* for attracting a new customer, client, or patient. Such a *system* seamlessly interconnects advertising (one or more types of it) with marketing and with selling, and possibly with conversion of a first-time buyer to a repeat or ongoing customer. None of these things thrive isolated on their own islands. Yet in most businesses and companies, this is exactly **the *system failure*** that occurs. Selling is left to the salespeople—after all, that's what they're getting paid to do, isn't it? Advertising is delegated to agencies, website developers, and social media "experts" (all of whom hate being held accountable for sales results). Marketing is a barely understood bridge between advertising and selling, often in serious neglect and disrepair and/ or staffed by people who also have other, separate jobs, so it is their bastard stepchild. If you become determined to organize these separated activities into an integrated *system*, you gain enormous advantages, but be forewarned: your efforts to do so will be mightily resisted, overtly and quietly undermined, by everybody living on separate islands.

***Operating systems* are the accepted norm and necessity**. Henry Ford revolutionized industry with *system* (the assembly line); Ray Kroc revolutionized—really created—"fast food" with *system* (McDonalds). Michael Gerber has brought countless entrepreneurs to the "altar of System" starting with his now-classic bestselling book

The E-Myth. Apple and Amazon have become two of the world's most valuable companies by their closed eco*systems*. My client, Richard James (therichardjames.com) tells lawyers he coaches: "*Systems* should run your practice; your people should run your systems."

Oddly, *marketing systems* are *not* the widely implemented norm. But they *are* found in the most successful businesses, small and large, and small grown to large. My own Magnetic Marketing System® and my system of "*Direct* Marketing for *Non*-Direct Marketing Businesses" have revolutionized the way top success is achieved and sustained in over two hundred different types of businesses. Advertising is made profitable by its incorporation into a complete marketing system. Another client of mine, Craig Proctor, craigproctor.com, for over a decade one of the top-ten ReMax real estate agents in the world, now the number-one business coach to high-income agents, has consistently made offline and online advertising pay off for agents (only) by having it feed into a comprehensive marketing *system*. Another client, Marty Fort (musicacademysuccess.com) makes every ad media—from radio and TV to direct-mail to Facebook—hugely profitable for his own music schools and for thousands of others' schools nationwide (only) by having that advertising feed a marketing *system*. This is the visible secret! **If you will let this book "springboard" you to making it a top priority to switch from just "advertising" to owning and operating a marketing *system*, you can revolutionize your business: less stress, more certainty, higher income without more quantity of work or hours, higher equity value for the day you wish to sell. To get started, go to MagneticMarketing.com/GetStarted.**

Advertising is best used to bring a potential customer, client, patient, member, subscriber, etc. through the first door into a hallway with rigid walls and a sequence of subsequent doors. Advertising tasked with doing more than this fails more often than not.

That first door is *expressed interest.* The potential customer steps over a literal or figurative threshold and agrees to engage in a conversation about your solution or opportunity, product or service, with a relatively open mind. But that's all he has done, and all he was asked to do by the advertising. This is an achievable goal for advertising, and you always want to be working with achievable goals.

Advertising *can also* discourage and screen out inappropriate potential customers at the same time it carries out the previously described purpose and mission. Fisher Investments' ads, for example, always include "if you have assets of more than $500,000."

Advertising can also "qualify" potential customers by having a "door charge," some (usually small) payment or first transaction, just to get in. A typical direct-response ad example is the free book offer, "just pay shipping and handling." For several years, I built a large business with free evening seminars for doctors, with "just a twenty-five-dollar refundable seat deposit required." Some online marketers refer to this tactic as having a "trip wire." It's set low, so no one with legitimate interest (worth investing your money and time in) is blocked, but it is enough to discourage those with no significant interest from clogging up your system.

For most small, local businesses and professional practices, and many national equivalents, this is the best use of advertising by far. Advertising can, of course, be tasked with carrying out a direct, completed sale, but make no mistake: this is harder, and a lot harder than it looks.

Either way, advertising should bring somebody through a door and deposit them in *a* seat on *a* forward moving ride, **a strictly *controlled marketing process.***

The important point from the above is the last three words: first, **controlled**. In a true system, there is very little if any flexibility. There is very little choice. If there seems to be choice, it is an illusion, like a magician's "card force." The person being put into your system has his thinking, movement, and behavior limited, focused, and controlled by you. That, for example, prohibits the dumb corporate website with all sorts of tabs and buttons to click on, letting the visitor wander about at his random choices as if a free-range chicken. Any web developer presenting you with such an abomination knows nothing about direct response, selling, system, or process. (You *might* have such a site for other purposes, but you would *never* drive first-time prospective customers, clients, or patients to it.) If your advertising is to succeed, it *can't* be influenced, let alone controlled, by any "technicians" or "mechanics" who know nothing about advertising to achieve your desired purposes. You have to tell them what you want, not the other way around.

Second, **process**. It starts with advertising (and earned media— i.e., publicity, public relations, media exposure, books, etc.) attracting appropriate prospects to *a* first entry point; *a* door. There may be many means of attracting prospects, but they should all deposit them at *one* door.

Incidentally, this is one of the very first innovations that Walt Disney introduced to the amusement park industry—from open, multiple points of entry to only one entrance and exit, so that the movement of every guest (customer) could be strictly controlled. What one sees first, second, and third, they *all* see first, second, and third. This is because it has been determined that there is a thing it is best for everybody to see first, and second, and third. Sydney Barrows and I coined a term for this: *Sales Choreography*. The "dance" of the prospective customer and the seller is not left to chance; each and every step of both participants is predetermined. It takes two to tango, but somebody has to lead.

There is *something* that influences and works better than other things, with every piece of the experience a potential customer has, such as the script for the answering of the phone, the order in which a person first tours a practice's office, etc., etc., etc. If speed of response to inquiry matters, then *every* person attracted by advertising gets sent their first package of requested information the very same day they ask for it—not as one of many handled once a week.

Sorry, but this puts the responsibility for design of process on you. If you bring in "experts" to help, be cautious, be demanding of relevant successful experience (not theory), then listen, consider, but ultimately you have to be Decider in Chief.

Third, about **marketing.** In a way, the entire experience the potential customer and the buyer have is a marketing process. But *marketing* is most important in two places: first, as the bridge between advertising and selling; second, after the first purchase, to cement satisfaction and develop the first-time buyer into a customer committed to ongoing or repeat activity and purchasing, and to acting as an enthusiastic "ambassador" and direct source of referrals.

Once advertising attracts, a multistep, multimedia marketing process should automatically occur, to prepare the potential customer for your sales event, whether it is in a physical setting or done at a distance, online or by phone.

This is *not* to feed lazy salespeople. It is, instead, to make good salespeople much more productive, profitable for you to employ, and easier to retain. Tasking a good *sales*person with cold prospecting or spending his time with poorly qualified, inappropriate, and ill-prepared prospects wastes his skill and talent and leads to cynicism and burnout.

"Content Marketing" Is a *Nonsensical* Term

In recent years, so-called "content marketing" has been popularized, even to the point of there being entire conferences about it, experts in it, and agencies specializing in doing it for you. For *most* businesses, it is bunk.

If you aren't in the publishing or entertainment business, you *aren't* in the content marketing business, and don't let anybody tell you that you are!

You have to focus on content *that sells.*

You don't actually market with "content," which would be content marketing. You may market with sales messages *disguised as* content. You may work at establishing authority, disguised as content. You may present criteria, a "quiz" or assessment tool, or "how to buy" rigged to your advantage and your competitors' disadvantage disguised as content. And so on. As a speaker (a human ad disguised as a "content speaker"), I often "taught" what to do and what not to do and provided checklists of marketing assets you need and should have (but likely didn't); I established my authority and the audience's inadequacy; but I never went so far as to (really) teach how to do it—yet it all *felt like* content to my audiences, and on large-audience, multispeaker events, I was consistently praised for delivering more content per minute than the others. I was a master of disguise! You should be too. It's a worthy ambition!

At Advantage, the home of longtime No BS | Magnetic Marketing member Adam Witty, along with Advantage and ForbesBooks publishers, we use the term "Authority Marketing." This is about "content" designed to create or bolster authority with a target market, meaning the power to prescribe (instead of having to sell). You can learn more about this Authority Marketing at authoritynow.com.

What I've termed Info-First Marketing is *very* different from "content marketing." The key word in mine is *first*. The "info" provided is just enough, as a first step, to get the prospect to the second step. I'm *not* interested in "content use statistics" like viral numbers, number of views, number of likes, blog audience, etc. except as it is *connected to movement* of potential buyers into and through a "funnel," onto a "ride" to a destination. To be emphatically, absolutely clear about this, *none* of the "information first" cast as bait and used to attract curious or interested potential customers is created, crafted, or provided to be informative or entertaining. That probably occurs, but only as by-product, in furtherance of the movement of the potential customer forward on a controlled path.

You have to decide what will "move" a prospect from attention, curiosity, and cautious optimism to a high level of interest, trust, and eagerness to hear your whole story, have a diagnostic or consultative conversation, and place himself in a sales situation. *Those* things, *that* information gets put into your *marketing process* bridging from advertising to selling.

To be entirely fair about this, there are businesses driven by what is now called content marketing. Toys and games are a great example. In 2019, all ten of the ten top-selling toy lines and eight of the ten top-selling video/online games were linked to TV, movie, and cartoon franchises and their characters. Hasbro, as a Disney licensee, had a blockbuster success with *Frozen II* toys and games. The movie, TV, and streaming "content" serves as (thinly disguised) indirect advertising for the toys and games, just as the toys and games serve as indirect advertising for the streaming, movies, and TV, as well as the theme parks. Disney perfected this closed loop at its very start and continues to this day. As owner of ABC, they regularly integrate Disney and Disney properties like Star Wars into ABC shows, and air Disney programming like its Christmas Parade—"content" and one long infomercial combined.

This is all well and good if and when useful for your business in accurately measurable ways, and you should always be intellectually curious, alert, and open minded about "nonadvertising advertising." *But, but, but* just because others are neck deep in pumping "content" out in blogs, social media, content-loaded web sites, YouTube videos, etc. does *not* mean it is productive for you, nor does their activity or its popularity mandate you doing it. Think of it this way: if your competitor across town or a business owned by an old college buddy suddenly hired one hundred new, additional employees, would you *reflexively, automatically* hire one hundred, too?

From Buyer to Customer

The other place that *marketing* creates an important bridge is after the first purchase. Most business owners count that as a victory at the end of a process, but really savvy operators recognize it as the start of the process of *conversion*. (By the way, rich people see starts where poor people see ends.)

This is about, first, erasing any postpurchase doubts and cementing satisfaction. If actual use of a product is required for that, then motivating and assisting with that use (with media) is part of this process. The billion-dollar acne "goop" brand that I helped develop advertising and marketing for, Guthy-Renker's PROACTIV®, was mostly sold for years by putting buyers into "forced continuity" (i.e., auto-charge, auto-ship of monthly supply), but control of cancellations was heavily dependent on getting the actual user (preteen, teen, or adult) to start using and stick with using it for enough days in a row to see results. This all had to be done at a distance, by media. I first learned about this "need" while still in my late teens in the Amway® business, about its Nutrilite® "super vitamins." Selling somebody the first month's supply was no victory; it was the first step of a process of in-person visits, drop-offs of another piece of literature, and phone calls every three days for twenty-one days to get use. Coincidentally, Bill Guthy and Greg Renker both had Amway® experience too.

Second, this is about **customer development**, so that they are committed ongoing or frequent repeat purchasers. You need fewer new customers if you very methodically increase the frequency of repeat purchase activity by existing customers. You should not feel entitled to maximum patronage because you do an excellent job with your deliverables; you should build and manage a marketing process to encourage frequency.

Conversion is, incidentally, a religious concept applicable to business. *Conversion* involves both commitment and evangelism. A converted customer is committed to the brand or business with its own patronage in its category and is an enthusiastic word-of-mouth advocate on its behalf to others. Business owners err in expecting this to happen on its own, by quality goods and services; it has to be purposefully engineered and managed as part of a complete marketing system. (My book *No B.S. Guide to Maximum Referrals and Customer Retention* addresses this in depth.)

If you start any type of engagement or participation with No BS|Magnetic Marketing, particularly a trial membership, you will see and experience a fairly involved conversion process timed out over the first thirty, sixty, and ninety days.

This is as good a place as any to mention the danger of assessing ads and ad campaigns by raw numbers (i.e., quantity of response, calls, even first transaction revenue). There is **the fact of *Differential* Value of Customers** to consider. Ad #1 or Media #1 could produce more front-end quantity but less back-end, long-term customer value than Ad or Media #2. Leads and buyers acquired from different ads and ad media need to be tagged and tracked over some set period of time to properly evaluate the comparative return on investment. As an example, I had a client who owned a productive, profitable full-page magazine ad I'd written for them, generating leads for a high-fee service, with a lot of potential back-end value in retained customers. One of the magazines he tested this proven ad in produced so little response he was eager to abandon it and did. But six months after the fact, close reexamination revealed two shockers: (a) the conversion rate from prospect to buyer to retained, active customer was much, much higher than that of "cheaper" leads generated in other media and (b) the six-month customer value was substantially higher as well. Over the next two years, the gap widened even further, making the leads produced from this (initially disappointing) media *the* best bargain in all of his advertising. Initial, raw numbers can often provide false positives and false negatives.

Here's a secret for you: advertising is really about (just) two things: behavioral psych and "money math." The richest entrepreneurs I know are very "into" both.

All of this is key to making advertising succeed rather than fail. **The very same advertising that is unprofitable when depositing potential customers into an environment with poor, disorganized, or nonexistent marketing systems can be magnificently profitable when depositing potential customers into a business with comprehensive, robust, well-run marketing systems.** Advertising can get people to buy, but it *can't* develop customers. That boldfaced sentence is important enough to stop, reread, and think about.

This is exactly why I developed my original Magnetic Marketing System®, which has now passed its thirty-year anniversary and has been the number-one bestselling marketing "toolkit" for business owners in the US and abroad. It is foundational to a complete portfolio of Magnetic Marketing advisory and support services, one-to-one coaching, and online resources provided by Magnetic Marketing. You can learn more without cost or obligation at magneticmarketing.com. You can also take a confidential marketing assessment, free. If you want to discuss your business with a Magnetic Marketing Advisor, you can set that up at the same website or call 800-871-0147. An offer also appears at the end of this book, on page 211.

I'm proud to say that Magnetic Marketing has transcended product or service or even philosophy to be a true *movement*, changing the way marketing is done by top producers and leaders in over two hundred different business categories and niches. Its most successful students and users have, in many cases, become teachers and coaches to their industries or professions. And their "star pupils" have also become thought leaders and teachers. Magnetic Marketing is well into its third generation of influence. This is *not* to suggest it is commonplace; it has moved from being radical to well-proven yet still relatively rare—as is success, period.

There are a couple of software companies, including ClickFunnels, originally birthed to automate and implement multistep, multimedia ad campaigns and full marketing systems. Setting up sales and marketing funnels along with automation used to be arduous and hard work. With a tool like ClickFunnels, and the training they provide, setting up a sophisticated Magnetic Marketing system and building the system for business is significantly easier than it's ever been. It's well worth the effort required and application in a business. You can learn more about it at ClickFunnels.com.

One more relevant "reveal": in my Renegade Millionaire System, I advance a vital premise: most business operators advertise to get a customer to make a sale, while Renegade Millionaires advertise to make sales to get (the opportunity to develop) customers.

Equity and security are relational, not transactional.

What *Is* Advertising, After All?

To look at all this another way, consider a night at the club, where singles go to mingle and hunt. She spends an hour or two getting herself "packaged" exactly as she intends, maybe very provocatively, maybe only mildly provocatively, maybe conservatively, depending on her purpose. He spends an hour getting himself "packaged," maybe trying to look very casual about the whole thing or maybe "peacocking," flamboyantly dressed. Both are engaged in advertising. Now, assume a match is made, and she goes to his place or vice versa. Certain expectations have been set. The appearances of the home, for example, are expected to be congruent with the advertising. If he advertised himself as a rich guy in expensive clothes and a Rolex watch, and his apartment is tiny and furnished in IKEA, he's got a problem. Or if she advertised as a sexual lioness, and her apartment is furnished like a grandmother's, and she has eight cats, problem. Things may deteriorate from there. **The reality is that *everything* is advertising *and a continuation of* advertising, and success requires *consistency*.**

The minute consistency starts to break down, by absence of seamless, organized process or by deviation from created expectations, trouble brews. And if your objective is relationship, not just a transaction(s), this is all the more important. Holding onto customers in a relationship requires advertising only what you can and will deliver, delivering on everything you stated or implied in advertising, and achieving integration of advertising, marketing, sales, and after-sale customer service and development. This mandates working forward with what will best attract and motivate customers—that, to be placed into your advertising, *and* working backward, with what you can and are willing to (systemize and constantly police so you can) deliver—thus restricting what you can place in your advertising.

The main reason I abandoned the ad agency and ad "creative" businesses very quickly, and repositioned myself as a marketing strategist, consultant, and copywriter is that I realized handing a client the best possible advertising wasn't effective or ethical; I needed to get my hands on the entire issue of consistency within his business. Brilliant but inconsistent advertising is *not* a good value for the client. Further, just to put a fine point on it, the traditional agency model ties the agency's income to getting the client to spend as much as possible on ad media, a clear and present danger for the client. My own business model tied my compensation to revenues brought in, not ad spend going out, and was rewarded for creating long-lived marketing assets and financial efficiency in the client's business. This incentivized me to meddle—and insist on consistency.

As the owner of a company, *you* have to insist on consistency (without me at your elbow, nagging about it). If you want your advertising to succeed instead of fail, *you* must succeed at achieving holistic integration of it with the entire relationship the customer will experience, and with your business's true and actual deliverables.

CHAPTER 5:

The Easiest Way to Guarantee That Your Advertising Never Fails Again!

By Darin Spindler: CMO Magnetic Marketing
| Cofounder KidsBowlFree.com

I'VE BEEN AN entrepreneur my entire life. My family built a small eight-lane bowling alley in a very small, rural central Wisconsin town the year before I was born. My grandparents owned a general store, a tavern, and a feed mill.

When I was in my early teens, I was able to attend some of the tradeshows and association meetings for the bowling industry. I'd sit in the front row taking notes about how to grow the business. The most fascinating thing to me about the events was how to create marketing materials or advertisements that attracted more bowlers to my parents' bowling alley.

At age fifteen I started a mobile DJ business and used some of the things I'd learned at those tradeshows to build up my DJ business. Each weekend I'd have a "gig" where I'd take my trailer and host a party—sometimes a wedding, other times a school dance or a fundraiser.

Little did I know that the principles of marketing and advertising were taught to my mentors from Dan Kennedy. I'd learn this about twenty years later when I became partner and cofounder of KidsBowlFree.com with my first business mentor, Bruce Davis.

Bruce was a student of Dan's and was teaching his direct-response principles to the bowling industry. I'm grateful that I picked up on what Bruce was teaching at such a young age, but it just made sense.

Market—Message—Media

Know who you want to attract.

Write a compelling message that gets the ideal prospect or customer to request more information from you, so that you can continue to follow up and build relationships. *This* is *the golden key that I'm going to share in my chapter.*

Then deploy your message via media.

Why Building Lists of Raving Fans and Ideal Prospects *Is* the Most Important Thing You Can Do

Let me share with you two stories about the value in building your list(s) and relationship with your list of ideal customers, clients, patients, subscribers, and Members.

I'll also share with you a simple system for building your own attraction-to-conversion system that can be deployed in hours.

In addition to KidsBowlFree.com and Magnetic Marketing, I'm also a partner in a restaurant in Green Bay, Wisconsin.

Before we even opened the restaurant, we started our birthday club. The concept was simple enough. Sign up for a *free* gift on your birthday, but we've built an entire system to generate steady sales from the list year round!

Many businesses keep waiting until they are open to start building up excitement about their business—a foolish mistake.

There are so many tools now available to your business to begin

> There are so many tools now available to your business to begin building buzz long before you open the front door of your business.

building buzz long before you open the front door or open the shopping cart of your website. Why struggle for the first few months or years, when you can build up anticipation and launch with a bang?

On our website we have a big banner that tells the visitor exactly how to get a *free* pizza on their birthday. The guest clicks and then they register by providing their name, email address, birthday, and phone number.

In return we'll give the guest a *free* ten-inch personal pizza valued at up to fifteen dollars on their birthday! This offer is only available by dining in, and it's rare that they dine alone. In fact this offer consistently generates more than twenty-one dollars for every one that's redeemed.

After a guest enters their initial information, then we ask for the guest's mailing address and then prompt them to share the birthday offer on their social media accounts or forward an email to a friend to sign up.

We also allow guests to register up to six family members, something we borrowed from my Kids Bowl Free program registration process.

We now have more than twenty-four thousand birthday club account holders and more than forty thousand guests that have a birthday in our system! This means that we get more than 1.5 people from each family registered.

It's important when you're investing money on Facebook, radio, TV, mail, and other media that you look for ways to leverage it. In this case we ask each main account holder to add additional birthdays to the system so we can create more visits from each family.

In addition to a banner on our website, we also have a specific landing page for registering. This is also an important asset to have. If you're unfamiliar it's just a webpage that has no navigation and only the ability to get the *free* information or in our case the *free* pizza that we're offering in the ads that we run to get traffic to this site.

Three Fast and Easy Ways We've Built Our List and You Can Too!

1. Facebook

2. Every Door Direct Mail

3. Newspaper Inserts

A SIMPLE WAY TO PUT FACEBOOK ADVERTISING ON AUTOPILOT TO HIT THE BULLSEYE EVERY TIME!

Let's cover Facebook first. In full disclosure I along with many other marketers have a very love/hate relationship with Zuckerberg, his minions, and his bots. For many businesses Facebook is a fabulous tool to help you attract a steady stream of customers, clients, and patients—in my experience especially for those who have hospitality or entertainment businesses.

I won't speak about all the other social media platforms, but they are all similar. They have audiences that you can access, and those platforms often know more about you than you know about you. Kind of creepy and scary in many respects.

… but we're capitalists and marketers.

So let's talk about how to profitably use Facebook.

For my restaurant we know our best customers are foodies, wine lovers, craft beer enthusiasts, vegans, and gluten-free fans!

We also know that our best guests are at least thirty years of age. I'm not saying that we don't have superfans under age thirty, but those who are older than thirty have more disposable income than those who are younger than thirty.

As a smart direct-response marketer and advertiser, you should always be looking for these biases in your business. If you have a limited amount of capital to deploy, how can you hit the bullseye every time? You need to know exactly what you're trying to hit or, in this case, attract.

As a smart direct-response marketer and advertiser, you also need to know who you want to repel. For our restaurant I have a special name for them. They are the five-dollar pizza customer. If someone is looking for a five-dollar pizza at one of the four or five big franchises that advertise this often, they are *not* my guest.

We don't spend a single penny trying to attract them. Do they sometimes show up? Yes. But if we get complaints or bad reviews, it's often from the five-dollar pizza customer who found us, tried it, and didn't appreciate the dough that we proof for three days in our coolers; the vegetables that we slice, chop, and roast; the meats that we make in house; or the incredible sauces and dressings we make with love from scratch each day.

The five-dollar pizza customer only really appreciates a low price, not a high-quality dining experience.

Facebook allows us to target exactly whom we want to attract.

For our restaurant we have a few custom audiences that we market to on a regular basis. If this term is new to you, just google it and locate the information on Facebook's site.

We also then have a few saved audiences that we target frequently with specific interests that include foodies, wine lovers, craft beer enthusiasts, vegans and gluten-free.

In our market there are about 250,000 Facebook accounts, but by narrowing it down with our ideal targets, we only advertise to about 40,000 of the 250,000 … ignoring 210,000 of the people who live in our community.

Facebook also gives us the ability to place ads in front of only ideal customers in the days leading up to their birthday!

Win!

And better yet, one of the things that Dan has taught all of us is to create an evergreen asset. The biggest challenge with social media is that it normally takes a lot of new creative on an ongoing basis, but by targeting only upcoming birthdays on Facebook, we can set that on autopilot.

For three years this campaign has been left untouched. It has a small daily budget for the ad, it targets only people whom we want to attract, and if you know more advanced Facebook advertising, we exclude all of our current birthday club members from seeing this ad.

This allows the ad to be mostly shown only to our ideal prospects, days before their birthday, and allows them to join the birthday club!

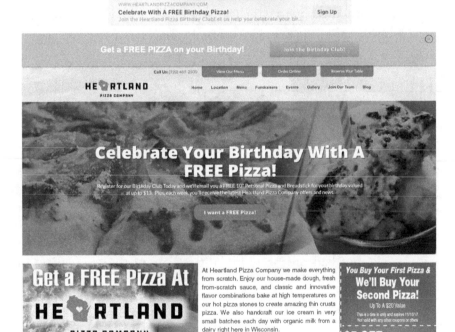

LET THE POST OFFICE DELIVER IDEAL CUSTOMERS TO YOU ON A SILVER PLATTER!

One of the tools that the post office has available that frankly few advertisers know about or use is Every Door Direct Mail (EDDM).

It's a pretty simple concept: you're able to deliver mailers to every door in a certain postal delivery route. Most of the routes in my community average about five hundred doors or mailboxes. The price to deliver is just under nineteen cents per home, rather than more than fifty-five cents for first-class postage.

This tool, like Facebook, is not for every job or every business. Like a construction project, a hammer is not the best tool for every project.

This tool allows you to target geographically with ease, as you pick the routes simply by clicking on the routes where you'd like to mail.

You're also able to target by household income to some degree as the USPS tool to print your postage actually shares a bunch of information like the average household income of the route that you're looking to mail to.

You can decide then, does this route deserve some of my advertising investment, or does it not?

At our restaurant, as an example, we have routes just around the corner from us with household incomes of around $50,000. Not bad people, but bad prospects for our restaurant that specializes in $20+ pizzas!

Just one route past them are a few neighborhoods where household incomes are $80,000 to over $110,000. In our community, these are the affluent neighborhoods, and they are ideal prospects.

We don't spend any of our advertising dollars in the $50,000 neighborhoods and opt to invest just two blocks away, where the ability to dine out is greater, and the homeowners also match much closer to our known categories of interest, including foodies, wine lovers, and craft beer enthusiasts.

Not nearly as scientific as Facebook, but with this advertising, we're putting the odds in our favor using known information and getting our same message to the prospects and customers in the mail.

You don't have to just mail postcards with Every Door Direct Mail either. They allow you to do some pretty sophisticated envelopes (up to 3.3 ounces at the time we publish this book) so long as they meet the weight and size requirements. My favorite, however, is to mail the largest-size postcard they allow, which is currently 15" x 12".

The reason I love this size is that 100 percent of the time I've done this, my postcard has been the wrap around all the other mail in the mailbox! Meaning that every envelope, magazine, brochure, and any other postcards are all wrapped by my mailer.

It's *impossible* to ignore, and frankly it's so big that in order to throw it in the trash, it usually needs to be ripped at least in half. We call it the *big ass* postcard, and it works.

It's an inexpensive way to stand out from the crowd with the prospects whom you want to attract to your business.

Often advertising fails and direct mail gets a bad rap because little thought is given to the format, how will your mail arrive, and how the guest will feel about getting it.

Before you send another piece of mail, start to think about *who* you're sending it to first, then *how* you'll deliver the message to give you the *best* chance at success.

THE NEWSPAPER MAY BE FADING, BUT IT'S NOT DEAD

Arguably the newspaper business is in decline from a print perspective, but it's not dead, and by considering the newspaper when others are fleeing the newspaper puts you in an advantageous position.

The less clutter, the better the odds that your message is seen, read, and responded to.

We've tested running display ads, those printed in the newspaper itself, mixed among the articles, and our results were less that we'd have hoped for.

But we didn't quit.

I've always wondered about the Sunday paper, where it was overflowing with coupons from grocery stores and furniture stores with the Sunday sale of the week.

As these are local business owners, often family owned, I couldn't imagine them just continuing to put in these complex advertisements week after week if they didn't work.

So we tested a Free Standing Insert (FSI) in the newspaper. You can get these on any day, but the Sunday subscription in my community, and I'm sure yours, is much higher than the daily delivery, so we opted to test on the highest number of readers.

We simply took our Every Door Direct Mailer, removed the postage, created new tracking URLs for our birthday club registration, and hit print! We then selected the routes that we wanted to attract customers from in our community, enough to hit the newspaper's minimum.

Now here's the surprising thing. You'd think inserting an 8.5x11 flyer into the paper would be more expensive than a one-eighth or one-quarter-page display ad, but it actually was quite a bit less expensive … and it was far more effective for us.

Now, as with all direct-response advertising, it may be different for you. Test it. For us we were able to drive traffic to the front door of the restaurant with an irresistible offer and then to our website to build our birthday club list.

Beyond Facebook, Mail, and the Newspaper ...

Over the past four years, we've used many other ways to grow our superfan list with our birthday club beyond Facebook, mail, and the newspaper.

As a smart direct-response advertiser and marketer, you should always be on the hunt for new places to grow your list(s).

We've done tradeshows and had giveaways. We've used Val-Pak, partnerships with radio stations, fundraising events.

They all had one common call to action.

Sign up for our birthday club and get a *free* pizza!

All of This Is Not About Giving Away *Free* Pizza ...

Many business owners are turned off by the word free, but they don't stop and think about what the cost of not having a list might mean to their business and their equity value.

For four years without fail, every Friday we send one email a week to our list to let our superfans know what's happening this week at the restaurant along with an offer.

It's not uncommon that in a given week 40 percent or more of our revenue comes from the list of superfans that we've built!

Your List Could Be Your Business's Lifeline

One of the most important and valuable lessons I've learned from Dan Kennedy isn't a marketing lesson, it's a simple quote: "Dig the well before you thirst." Be prepared!

In March of 2020, when government agencies at the flip of a switch made everyone shelter in place, and nobody could go to work, the mall, or nearly anywhere, most businesses panicked. Yes, it was frightening for businesses.

If nobody was out working, who'd be able to dine at your restaurant? If families couldn't leave their homes for a great weekend dining out, how could you keep your employees working and your bills paid?

Because we had been building our customer and prospect list every day for more than three years at the time, we had the ability to quickly and frequently communicate with our guests. We were able to inform them that we made the decision to get in the delivery business, when we had previously depended upon services like UberEats and GrubHub, which allowed us to keep all of our team working and improve our experience and margins.

But we had been digging our well for more than three years.

Early in the pandemic we increased our email communication from once a week to twice a week, allowing us to update guests with new things we were doing to provide them a great meal and keep us ringing the cash register.

We also did some interesting things: we offered our dressings for takeout, we created cookie kits, we offered a Zoom pizza class at home. Guests picked up the entire kit at the restaurant, and we did a Zoom class where we taught them how to throw dough and make a pizza.

In the first twelve weeks after the initial lockdown, we had some of the best weeks in our company history—without a single guest dining in and not a single party in our party space.

All because we have the ability to quickly communicate and make creative offers.

Compare this to the experience of most restaurants during the early days of the pandemic. Many laid every employee off and now a year later are finding it really difficult to get their team back to work.

But many just locked the doors. They were 100 percent dependent upon traffic coming to their strip mall or shopping mall, and when there was literally no traffic to grab, they were up the creek without a paddle.

Many of the businesses have been around since before my restaurant. Many of them are franchises or corporate stores with much deeper pockets to develop systems like I've just described.

Golden Opportunities to Generate Cash Surges, at Will, in Ten Minutes or Less

When you own your list, you have the ability to ring the register at will. As the pandemic continued into the fall and winter, our restaurant, which is near seven hotels in Green Bay, needed to figure out how to capture some of the lost revenue that we normally take in from the Green Bay Packers home games.

When you own your list, you have the ability to ring the register at will.

If you're not a football fan, game day in Green Bay is a *big* deal. The city essentially doubles in size for the ten games hosted here each year. We only have season tickets, and they are sold out, with a waiting list large enough to fill the stadium a second time. Fans wait decades to get their season tickets.

I look at this traffic to our business as the cherry on top of the sundae, not our business. Some businesses come to depend upon big events, big conventions, etc. and never build a loyal fan base, opting for the "easy" tourist money or business event money, and the pandemic exposed this lazy way of thinking.

If you're dependent upon traffic from another business or large events instead of being proactive to advertise, attract, and nurture your own superfan base, you are dependent, not independent. The power in business comes from being independent.

In early September I was at my Florida home and decided that on game day, since we had no fans in town, and it would be hard to generate revenue like we normally would do from September to December without the ten big weekends we have when the Packers are in town, we'd have to do something *big*.

For the first game of the year, we decided to send out a Buy One, Get One *Free* pizza offer to our list of superfans. The offer was valid for an hour before the game to an hour after the game.

Within minutes of sending the first email, the orders began to pour in. In fact it was so successful that we beat our Sunday numbers in 2019 when we had nearly one hundred thousand fans in town for the game! We needed to have four delivery drivers working.

If you find a winner, you repeat it. We continued to do this offer throughout the season, even on the away games as our local superfans loved the offer, and it kept the dough coming in the register and the dough going out the doors to our superfans!

Amplify Your Email on Facebook

Building a list like this also allows you to use additional media like Facebook to then amplify your message.

After we write an email, we can quickly and easily turn that message into a Facebook post with text and a photo, and then we can run a relatively small budget ad to our email list.

Most won't open our emails. Even if you're a superstar with your emails, it's likely you get 40 percent of them opened at best. Meaning more than 60 percent are not seeing your message. Most businesses are now experiencing open rates under 20 percent, so using this second step helps get in front of your email subscribers in a place where many of them spend a lot of time: on Facebook.

If you've not uploaded audiences to Facebook before, I'll guide you through it in a special *free* video and talk you through how to create a few audiences for you to run simple ads at the end of this chapter.

In addition to just posting with text, you may actually want to pull out your cell phone and create a live video with the same message and then promote it instead of using text and photos. It's best to mix up what you post: some videos, great photos, and make sure you have good copy.

In 2021 when this book is being released, it seems that authentic videos and great photography are what is getting most social media users to stop the scroll.

Make Your Advertising and Marketing Unstoppable!

You can see how I've built a *system* for building a brick-and-mortar business.

Advertise a great offer in a variety of media. In this case it's a *free* pizza on your birthday.

Provide a place for the ideal prospect to join your list or download your app. We now have more than seven thousand users of our app too! This list is even more valuable than our email list, as they are all guests who've ordered through us, but we built this list sending traffic to it from our emails.

Do you see how this is all connected?

With the list, you have power.

Without the list, you're powerless.

I can't imagine the sleepless nights that I'd have if I didn't have lists of my guests and prospects for the various businesses that I'm invested in.

When you have a list(s) and you build relationships with your customers, clients, and patients, you're unstoppable even when faced with a global pandemic!

DARIN SPINDLER is a Magnetic Marketing legend and is widely known for his complex marketing systems and his ability to get a lot done fast. Darin was awarded the 2008 Glazer Kennedy Insider's Circle Implementer of the Year. Darin is a contributing author to the *NO B.S. Price Strategy* book with Dan Kennedy, the millionaire-maker. Darin is the cofounder of KidsBowlFree.com and has helped to create over thirty million new customers for bowling centers around the globe. Darin also has a done-for-you marketing services company that provides bowling centers, CoolSculpting salons, and spas along with a handful of private clients. Darin is also the founder of Heartland Pizza Company in Green Bay, Wisconsin. Darin used direct marketing to fuel every business that he's invested in, both online and offline. In addition to his business interests Darin is the proud father of Presley, named after her mother's love of Elvis. Darin is also a five-time Ironman finisher and is hoping to get to Kona someday.

GET *FREE* VIDEO LESSONS FROM DARIN AND DOWNLOAD A COUPLE OF THE MOST SUCCESSFUL ADS SHARED IN THIS CHAPTER ...

I've created a short video for you at DarinSpindler.com/WAF where I'll show you how to use the EDDM tool, simple Facebook advertising and targeting strategies, and more tools to make your advertising successful!

DarinSpindler.com/WAF

CHAPTER 6:

The Big Lie

THERE ARE A LOT of big lies in life and in business, like the check is in the mail … I'm from the government, and I'm here to help … it's not you; it's me. You really have to be on guard against this one: new or different media requires new or different strategies, tactics, and messaging. This *big lie* is how "experts" and agencies sell themselves while evading accountability. It is mysticism. They argue new "culture," new rules and new metrics, but **there is only one metric you're allowed to put on a bank deposit slip: money made**. The banks won't let you deposit views, viral views, "likes," comments, stars, etc. from online media any more than they'll accept "pass along" statistics or Nielsen ratings from print or broadcast media. Only money made. This requires you to be resolute, even ruthless about measurement in ROI—return on investment—counted in dollars.

The "culture" argument for different media is utter and complete nonsense. An ad message is either compelling and magnetic or it isn't. What works is what works, period. **There are *essentials* for ad** messages that *never* change regardless of the media involved—whether handbills stapled to telephone poles at stoplight intersections or website landing pages or YouTube videos. (See chapter 7: Ad Message Essentials.) Anybody who tells you that these essentials are "culturally inappropriate" for *any* media is either a fool or a liar. Period. End of story. And if there is a media where you are prohibited from using an effective message constructed with these essentials, you should avoid it. Period. End of story.

What Do *You* Want in *Your* Pond?

Success with *anything*, including but not limited to advertising, is rarely forced on somebody. It is a lot less accidental than most people like to think—because it being a matter of luck or fate relieves them of personal responsibility. Instead, it is the sum total, from adding up choices made. This is not to *entirely* deny luck as a factor. I was lucky to have been born in America versus any number of other far less advantageous places, lucky with the parents I got, lucky to find the wife I'm married to, and so on—although that third one required more than luck. But if you dissect most successes—individuals', companies'—and isolate each causative factor, and you are honest about it, you'll find "choices made" the number-one most important success factor. This is the truth behind my statement: *Your customers are* your *fault*.

Paul J. Meyer, a highly successful insurance industry entrepreneur, then founder of Success Motivation Institute and author of the "Dynamics of Goal-Setting" course that I studied when just starting out, succinctly summarized a key truth of achievement versus disappointment and frustration: "If you are not getting what you want, it is probably because your goals are poorly defined." *Clarity* is extremely powerful. This is true, specifically, with customer acquisition: if you are not getting the customers you want (thus getting customers you don't want or who are of poor value), the problem probably starts with your goal(s) about those customers being poorly defined; with lack of clarity about the desired customer; and then with using advertising messages and/or media not precisely matched to a precisely defined, desired customer.

Advertising might seem to be about technical choices: what media to use in what way, how much to spend in one media versus another, and so on. All significant, but in a bigger context: it's important to understand that **you *choose* your customers**, and that starts with the advertising you use to attract them. You decide, proactively or by default, what winds up in your pond. Luck does *not* make that decision for you.

There is a scene in the terrific HBO series *Deadwood*, with the two rival bar and whorehouse operators discussing one's recent addition of craps tables. He is bemoaning the

> You should think about all advertising decisions in this context: *Is this crafted and aimed to attract the customer I want?*

fact that his customers are proving too damn dumb to play the game. It is arguable he had no choice in his customers, stuck in an isolated frontier town—but you do. I often catch a business owner complaining about his customers—dumb, cheapskates, bargain hunters, of poor long-term value, etc.—and I am quick to insist that he *chose* those customers. You should **think about all advertising decisions in this context: *Is this crafted and aimed to attract the customer I want?***

This specifically applies to *length of copy*, whether delivered online, in pages or in video, and offline, in print ads or direct mail.

Longer almost always outperforms shorter, unless it's (a) boring or (b) poorly matched with the audience asked to give it their attention and time. You will hear the case for very brief made by referencing a declining attention span, reducing the average human's attention capability to that of a goldfish: seven to seventeen seconds, and at most seven minutes. I ask: Even if true, are you sure you want the *average* human as your customer? (Dumb and broke.) Are you attempting to get *goldfish* as your customers?

Be careful here. And regarding "brevity required," consider all the proof to the contrary. Large audiences watch *thirty-minute* competition shows about building things with Lego blocks and baking cupcakes and even still watch and support *thirty-minute* infomercials (ads) selling skin-care products, "miracle" mops, investing in gold coins and bullion, and "amazing" fishing lures and golf clubs.

The most successful strategy I have repeatedly used for selling via online webinars involves up to several hours of sequential ten- to thirty-minute video ads, bringing people through a door to register for and then (get follow-up marketing to) attend a three- to four-*hour* *"live"* webcast. By the time they get a hard offer and can and do buy, they may have from three to seven hours invested. The most successful online webinar (slides with voice-over plus video clips) that I ever wrote was forty-six minutes long and lived for the client for seven years of continuous use, with traffic driven to it daily. Such lengths are chosen based on optimum time to make a particular sale to an appropriate, interested audience—not to satisfy some predetermined "cultural rules" or arbitrary limits.

Remember early in this book I used the unflattering term "advertising *victim*"? If you let yourself be persuaded or bullied into investing *your* money in some wizard's insisted-upon abandonment of either effective ad messaging or dollar-based, return-on-investment accountability, you *are* being victimized. But as my friend and colleague Lee Milteer[3] says, "There are no victims—only volunteers." Ultimately, your customers are your fault.

Personally, I have made myself fortunate in this regard most of my life: I have successfully attracted customers and clients I genuinely like and respect. I have had to spend very little time dealing with people who don't appreciate and respect me. I have stubbornly refused randomness. I have taught others in a myriad of different businesses to start with this as a principle, then develop strategies and tactics in harmony with it.

Look, don't be a dope. Don't advertise just because you think you should, because others do, defensively in reaction to competitors, randomly, or only desperately against sales slumps. Learn to advertise to support a complete "scheme" of goals and objectives, not the least of which might be the "nature" of the customers you attract and subsequently live with.

---

3   Lee Milteer is a celebrated peak performance coach specializing in getting and keeping entrepreneurs thinking accurately, staying focused on activities that legitimately "move the needle," and creatively managing change. Her work can be found at milteer.com.

CHAPTER 7:

Ad Message *Essentials*

THIS CHAPTER, BY ITSELF, can guide your development of advertising.

There are essential elements for just about everything. For us: air we can breathe, water we can drink, food we can eat and derive nutrition from, and safe shelter we can protect. This has *not changed* since we lived in caves, even before the high-tech inventions of hinged doors, fire, and refrigeration. It won't either. For enduring relationships, essentials are mutual respect, trust, and common interest or purpose. Nothing will change that, not even an app. The very use of "essential" is meant to apply to such things *not* subject to change, so it shouldn't be used casually. And I do not.

Here are the four essential elements of an advertising message with a reasonable opportunity of being successful. There are other optional elements; there are other useful and powerful elements, but these are the four absolute essentials.

One of the most harmful aspects of Hillary Clinton's 2016 presidential campaign was her lack of a great answer to this. Hers, basically, was "Because *I want* to be president; it's *my* turn, dammit; *I'm* a Clinton, dammit; and my opponent is a buffoon." To women, her case was "You *have to* vote for me because I'm a woman." Biden made a nearly identical mistake with the African American population in 2020, at one point actually saying out loud, "If you're confused about whether to vote for me or Trump, you ain't black" (i.e., "You *have to* vote for me.") None of this answers "Why you?" *from the perspective of the customer.* To Hillary's surprise, these voters refused to behave "properly," as they were "supposed to," as they were obligated to do. Joe survived the same error, barely, basically by hiding out and avoiding the question as much as possible—letting Trump run against Trump, against COVID-19, and against the media. You probably won't get to hide and have others carry all your water for you, so you'd best develop really, really good answers to these questions.

Rhino Shield House Paint makes its case, in part, this way:

Our *unique* ceramic coating means *you* will never need to paint your house again, and ten years from now it will look like it was just painted—guaranteed.

I am assuming having your house painted with Rhino Shield costs significantly more than with ordinary paint, but the value proposition is in saving money over time and having a more valuable, saleable home should you move on. Theirs is an argument of **"legitimate and specific difference,"** rather than the vague, unspecific, and me-too premises of most advertising. This is also about "Lead the Field," by defining a new and different field altogether. In ad lingo, this is sometimes referred to as "category of one" positioning.

The USP or UVP is *not* to be confused with a mere slogan. It *might be* expressed as a slogan—in its formative years as a new, unique, and amazing service Federal Express's "Absolutely, Positively Overnight" worked just fine. Sadly, most slogans are toothless, vague, "cute," and /or easily used by competitors. "Our Customers Are Family" or "Quality, Value & Service For 25 Years" have *no* impact.

Even long-enduring, theoretically "good" ad slogans deserve skepticism about their true effectiveness. Only once to my knowledge, an ad copywriter was referenced by name as part of a clue on *Jeopardy*, in April 2020, given credit for the famous slogan of "a major financial services firm." The correct slogan was first written up in 1999, and is still in use: "What's in Your Wallet?" Two of the three *Jeopardy* contestants got it right, as did I. But it's probably a good thing they weren't required to also name the company, Capital One. In a brand awareness survey, a full 40 percent of respondents assigned the slogan to Visa, another 10 percent to MasterCard. *Ooops.*

Expressed, **legitimate and specific difference** triumphs over mere cleverness. It is a good discipline to impose on your ad messaging, even including a USP, UVP, or slogan, and it is a good demand to impose on your business—a valid reason for you existing in the marketplace (other than your desire to be there and your need for revenue).

As a brief divergence, I'd like to caution you about a common disappointment and frustration about "the mind of money," and why it moves from one person or business to another: **money is unresponsive to *need*.** Your needs held in your mind and carried into the way you advertise your business have *zero* attraction to money; they are utterly unpersuasive to the marketplace. You must have and then advertise far better reasons for your taking up space in a marketplace than the fact that you've always wanted to own a bakery, now you do, and you need customers to pay the rent. You must have better reasons than just being there as another bakery. **The marketplace is brutal in its rejection of "another" and "ordinary."** Do *not* expect it to "give bulant sloth settled onto his couch for the duration, but your ad compels him to leap up and rush to his telephone or computer to respond immediately. If your call to action isn't *that* clear, *that* compelling, and *that* urgent, head back to the drawing board; more work is needed.

Two key points about this:

Point #1: Most business owners *incorrectly* think about their advertising as being about their products and services when, in reality, it needs to be about its intended audience plus "behavioral psychology." Such behavioral psych factors as FOMO: fear of missing out; safety in numbers; scarcity = urgency; ego and identity (I am because I own "X"), etc. drive response universally, regardless of the product or service, far more than will the attributes of a product or service. This is why it is so important to know a lot about your customers and desired customers, not just a lot about your products and services. In consulting, I can usually stump a business owner or CEO with my first three questions about his own customers, clients, or patients. He may hold assumptions, but I reveal that he has few if any facts and only superficial understanding.

Your advertising has an exponentially better chance of success if you can recite verbatim, as if writing a play, these three conversations of your customers:

1. At the kitchen table at dinner

2. At the kitchen table, in the middle of the night when one spouse who couldn't sleep has come downstairs and the other notices, follows, and insists on knowing what's bothering him or her

3. In the car, on the way home from an afternoon or evening at their adult children's house

For B2B advertising, a similar list applies.

By the way, one of the most interesting leaders in marrying behavioral psych with advertising (and marketing and public relations) was Edward Bernays, a nephew of Sigmund Freud. One of Bernays's books, *Propaganda*, is readily available and well worth reading.

Point #2: **People *cannot* be relied on to act on their needs or desires or in their own best interests, especially in a timely manner, without "a firm hand" guiding them.** Almost all advertisers give too much credit to *their* customers or clients or patients. But this is their own ego talking. Because of this, they omit the specific call to action.

The call to action is what separates direct response from all other perambulations of advertising and separates the courageous advertisers from the cowards. The timid may *inherit* the earth, but in the here and now, fortune favors the bold. ***Call to action cowardice* castrates an otherwise effective advertisement.**

CHAPTER 8:

How to Attract More High-Paying Clients and Close Big Fat Deals Using Sales Consultations

By Robin Robins, Founder of Technology Marketing
Toolkit, MSP Success Magazine, and Big Red Media

IF YOU ARE a business or professional that sells by driving prospects to some type of sales consultation, this chapter will be of great utility for you, showing you how to double, possibly triple, the number of clients to you efficiently, cost effectively, and without a ton of manual labor and brute force selling. It will also provide the added benefit of being able to close a higher percentage even at a higher price point.

How can I make such an audacious claim? Because about ten years ago, with Dan Kennedy's help, I figured out how to build and scale a sales consultation process for my business that has consistently driven no less than two thousand new client consultations every year with as close to a "set it and forget it" process as any true-blue marketer could hope for.

Further, I've done this for thousands of my clients, who are companies selling IT services, solutions, and support, helping them quite literally quadruple the number of new client appointments they get over the industry average, close at a higher rate, *and* at higher fees than industry peers.

But before we dig into the secret sauce, and staying true to the theme of this book, I want to give you the disclaimer that this won't be easy to set up and get cranking. Will it be worth it? You betcha. And the best analogy is found in the old story of the two villages ...

Two neighboring villages were getting their fresh water from a nearby well. Every morning, the people would wake up, grab their buckets, and make the journey to the well to get clean, fresh water. It worked, it was simple, but it was also labor intensive. If one family member was ill or injured, they had to depend on the kindness of others or go without water. If the weather was bad, they wouldn't be able to make the journey. If there was no rain, the well water would get low, and not as much water would be available. And during the summer months, they had to make multiple trips to get sufficient water for their gardens and livestock.

Then one day, one of the village leaders had an idea for building a pipeline system that would deliver fresh water on demand without buckets and without manual labor. He shared the idea with the neighboring village, but they cringed at the heavy cost, time, and labor involved in building it. They didn't like that they would have to continue the bucket brigade *while also* putting in the money and effort to build a water pipeline. They had never done anything like this before and were afraid they could do all the work, invest a considerable amount of money, and run the risk of it not working or requiring a lot of troubleshooting. So, the leader of that village declined, saying they would stay with the current system, which was simple, easy, inexpensive, and working "good enough."

After the pipeline was built, the village that built it was thriving, having fresh water on tap whenever they needed, freeing them up from carrying buckets to build bigger and stronger infrastructure and develop the village. Their crops flourished because they eliminated drought. Their farm animals were healthier because they always had fresh water. The village eliminated a number of diseases and sicknesses because their water was cleaner, and they had the ability to build sanitation systems that flushed sewage far away from the village. They were able to save up water for times when the rain didn't come, and the people were happier and healthier as a result.

The other village? Well, things stayed exactly the same, except that many of the smart villagers left and moved to the neighboring village, reducing their manpower. They had some good days, but many bad ones, and still they stubbornly refused to replicate what the neighboring village had done, convinced it was "too much work" and "too much money." Besides, it would break tradition! They were also skeptical that such a system would work in their village because their village "was different." They didn't have the money and strong labor the other village had, especially now that the other village had recruited some of their best and brightest. They couldn't afford to take men from the bucket brigade to build a pipeline. They never progressed, never improved, only getting more bitter and resentful of the other village, blaming them for their own failures.

Sound familiar?

It's the story of so many businesses that are small and struggling but then stubbornly choose to stay small and struggling. They shy away from anything that takes time and money, essentially starving their business from the fuel it needs to grow. So, you should know in advance that the system I've built won't come "cheap" or easy. Cheap and easy is putting a phone number or Contact Us form on your website and having that lead just go to your inbox or voice mail, where you manually chase them down to book the appointment. Maybe they book the consultation, maybe they don't. The end.

Anyone can run that simple process, and most do—which is why roughly 80 percent of businesses in America never break the $1 million mark, and less than .5 percent ever get beyond $10 million. Even in the IT space, where the need for cybersecurity solutions is high, the services are sold on a "subscription" basis, the average client value runs into the thousands, and the people running the business are no stranger to technology and automation, 79 percent of them never break the $1 million mark.

That's because they are averse to complexity—and there are no simple solutions to complex problems.

As Uncle Dan always said, **most business owners grossly underestimate the difficulty of the task of getting a profitable new client in the door** and therefore do "some" of the work but not *all* of the work required, looking for the cheapest way to do something, which leaves them frustrated and disappointed with the poor performance of their marketing efforts. But instead of doubling down on the sophistication, effort, and investment to fix what's not working, they brush it off as "that didn't work" (speaking of a specific campaign) or "*this* doesn't work," dismissing an entire category of marketing altogether (Facebook, SEO, direct mail, or whatever), which causes them to stop doing everything, sliding them back to square one, where they repeat the process over and over again, getting nowhere, learning nothing and making no progress.

So, if you're still with me, let's dig in.

The Core Fundamentals of Lead Generation (a Review)

To get a prospect to raise their hand and show interest in doing business with you, which is a sales lead, you have to give the prospect a good reason to want to engage with you. We call this lead generation marketing.

However, if the *only* reason you give for responding is something like "We do _____. We're really, really good. We might be even better than your current company/provider/person. Come on. Give us a shot," **you won't motivate anyone other than the most desperate, ready-to-buy prospects to call you—and those prospects will also need to meet the following criteria:**

1. They would need to have already decided they want to buy what you're selling.

2. They would need to be convinced to buy it from *you* over all other competitors.

3. They would need to be ready to buy right now.

That's a lot of contingencies, which means we are unlikely to get very many leads. The simple reality is there aren't that many "buy-now buyers" out there, and even fewer who know who you are. As a society, we're overrun with available choices and options.

So, by making an offer, we can start the process of list building and setting up a pipeline of "getting-ready-to-buy buyers" in our sales funnel that will lead to a sales consultation.

How to Craft an Offer

There are two big, general categories of offers: The first is some type of *free information*. The second is the *free consultation*. There are a number of ways (media) to offer free information that range from a free report to an in-person seminar. If you are unsure about where to start, I highly recommend you create a buyer's guide to what you sell that sets the criteria for what "good" is.

> There are two big, general categories of offers: The first is some type of *free information.* The second is the *free consultation.*

For example, most of you reading this are not savvy IT people (nor am I, for that matter). So, if you are looking to hire an IT consultant for a project or to support your computer network, how do you determine who is knowledgeable, is honest, and can be relied on to do a great job, and who is grossly incapable of handling the job you need done? What questions should you ask to ferret out the unethical and incompetent IT people who will royally screw everything up, overcharge you, and not follow through? Do *you* even know what "good" IT support is and what it should cost?

Probably not. That's why I coach my clients to offer a buyer's guide to how to find a competent IT pro. One of the reports they offer is titled "21 Critical Questions You Should Ask Your Next IT Consultant before Signing a Contract to Avoid Being Ripped Off, Overcharged and Left with a Giant Mess."

If you were starting to look for an IT company, that report would be of great interest to you—which is exactly what we want to happen.

Here's a *short* list of ways to offer *free information*:

- Free guide, report, white paper, etc.

- Audio/podcast (someone interviewing you on a topic)

- Video

- Book—hard copy or e-book

- Checklist or cheat sheet (Compliance Checklist for IT Directors of Medical Practices)

- Quiz to determine something (think *Cosmo* quiz or personality-type quizzes)

- In-person seminar, webinar

Similarly, a "free consultation" is essentially a sales appointment. We don't call it a "sales appointment" because we're marketers, and we want to entice a prospect to us, not scare them away. Therefore, we call it something interesting, like (in the IT world) a "Cyber Security Risk Assessment," to know for sure if your computer systems and data truly are secure from ransomware, hackers, rogue employees, and countless other hazards.

Here's a short list of "consultation" offers you can make:

- First service call free

- Free diagnostic test/scan

- Assessment, "tune-up," or health check

- Gift with initial appointment

- Free trial (start for free, pay only after X days, satisfied, etc.)

- Competitive bid (compare us to what you pay now)

- Contests, sweepstakes, draw

- "Scholarship" application or funding for a project

offer in spring and summer, LOL). That's why a free assessment can be a valuable offer—you don't need to have an immediate problem to say yes.

2. **Whatever you give away should provide *real* value.** Don't peddle nonsense and useless information, or a consultation that is nothing more than your standard sales pitch. All you'll accomplish by doing that is to convince a prospect that your services are just as useless, and they will feel duped if you promoted the information or consultation as something other than a sales pitch. This ties into my principle of always providing **value in advance**. If you want more prospects to meet with you, answer this question: How will they benefit from meeting with you even if they don't buy? *Put some serious thought into this.* What can you deliver? How can you benefit them? How can *you* provide "value in advance"?

3. **Promoting free information is the correct offer to make when you can't provide a lot of copy.** For example, if I'm running a Facebook ad, it's a lot easier to create an ad that sells a free webinar, book, or report, because the title will essentially sell it (see above). For the ad to work, I need a solid headline and a picture of the thing I'm giving away. But if I'm offering a free consultation, I need to do more value build, talk about what it is and why they need it, answer questions, and provide details on "how it works" and "what will happen."

4. **Whatever you give away as free information *must accomplish two things*.** *First*, the information must be a *carefully constructed* "sales letter" that *builds* interest in doing business with you by also creating dissatisfaction with their current

provider/situation and *selling them on taking the next step of booking a consultation with you.* Otherwise, you're wasting your time putting together free information. For example, I see vendors in our industry promoting guides titled "The Ultimate Guide to Marketing for MSPs" or similar. Of course, I download those to see what they're up to (LOL) and whether there's anything I can learn or glean (always a student). Problem is, the report has *nothing* to do with buying their products and services, which are not marketing services but some type of software or tool for service delivery. Because of this, it falls apart like a cheap suit at the end, where it should be convincing you to take the next step toward buying from them—be it signing up for a demo, a free trial, or at least a one-on-one consultation.

Second, it also must position *you* as the go-to expert, building trust and establishing your credibility, eliminating all other options.

5. **If you create a "free information" offer that works, you can get more play with it by simply changing the media in which it's delivered.** For example, I conducted a webinar titled "6 Ways to Get More High-Paying Clients without Spending a Dime on Marketing." That webinar performed so well that we turned it into an evergreen webinar, then got it transcribed and made into an e-book, then an on-demand video. Each version (media) attracted different prospects, even though the title of it and its contents were the same. That's because some people won't watch a video but will register for a webinar. Some prefer a book or written guide. So, if you strike upon a presentation that sells, convert it to a report. If you strike upon a report that works, turn it into

a webinar. Doing so will give you more play and more leads from different people without starting from scratch.

6. To convert those who requested the free information to a qualified appointment (consultation), you need **fast, multimedia follow-up** (calls, emails, direct mail) that sells the prospect on booking the consultation. (See the opening of this chapter regarding the high-level overview of what has to happen when a lead comes in.)

Again, let me *stress* this critical point: the free "information" should be strategically written, crafted, and designed to *sell them on doing business with you*—but it has to be done in a manner that feels educational. That teaches them something and (again) provides value.

I often get IT company CEOs coming to me for help after conducting a presentation or webinar where they spoke to a sizable crowd but didn't generate any leads or appointments. They want to know what to do now to corral the herd. My advice is always the same: get in a time capsule and go back to before the event and design your presentation to drive those people to the back of the room to either buy something or at least book a consultation at the point when they were *most* likely to do that (at the end of your presentation). *They* made the mistake of thinking all they had to do was put on a "show" about ransomware or how to spot a phishing email. Wrong.

Candidly, the art of designing such a presentation or free information that actually does educate them but also sells is a high-level skill, and you want to find someone who can do a great job at this.

Marketing a Free Consultation

The concept of offering a "free consultation" is a staple for businesses selling *complex* solutions. Doctors, financial advisors, CPAs, and lawyers all drive prospects to a consultation to close them on their services. They, like the IT companies I work with, need to *prescribe a solution.* They're not offering "add to cart" IT services on their website. Even if they did, no intelligent person or cold prospect would buy it, and in many cases, selling an "off-the-shelf," one-size-fits-all service without proper diagnostic evaluation would be malpractice if not downright unethical.

My guess is that you are already selling by consultation, **but the process is wildly erratic, random, and unplanned**. Lead comes in. You get on the phone (if you can get them on the phone). You say whatever comes to mind, and the entire process is arbitrary, based on how you feel that day. Or how the prospect feels. They decide. Some close, some don't. No process, no system, no agenda, no preparation. It either moves forward or it doesn't. The questions you ask and the dialogue you have aren't planned in advance. There's no preselling happening before the call to properly prepare a prospect using a quality shock-and-awe box and presales appointment marketing system.

If your inbound lead "process" is akin to free-range chicken running around in a yard, I guarantee you're leaving a *lot* of money on the table. It's also (most likely) frustrating at least some of your prospects and ruining your reputation because a prospect who senses you're all over

> Map out the process, from what that prospect receives before they meet with you, to what you actually say and do during the consultation.

the map in the initial sales meeting will assume your entire business is that way (and they might be right—how you do anything is how you do everything).

So, the first *big* lesson here is to map out the process, from what that prospect receives before they meet with you, to what you actually say and do during the consultation. Be sure to address the most common concerns and objections *in advance* so they don't come up in the sales meeting.

Price is always one objection salespeople complain about. So, if you *are* the most expensive provider in your area (or at least not the cheapest), you should address that in advance of the consultation (sales meeting) and reiterate it early on in the process.

An example: "We decided a long time ago we'd rather explain why our prices are roughly 10 to 20 percent higher than those of all the other IT firms in our area than cut our prices and services and apologize for poor services every day thereafter. The reason we're more is because we hire more techs per client, which means you'll get faster response to any problems you're having. We also don't outsource our support to overseas countries where the workers are cheaper but are a big unknown—and in today's risky cybersecurity world, we feel far more comfortable and confident that our consultants be on US soil and people we employ rather than strangers in a cubicle whom we've never met. We also invest heavily in our technicians' education and skills and pay more for top talent rather than trying to get by with the cheaper talent out there. All of this costs more, but our clients are those who are willing to pay a bit more and get white-glove service they can trust rather than save a few dollars but have problems, downtime, lost data, and the threat of a ransomware attack hanging over their head, hoping nothing will happen."

Now, here are a few key strategies to keep in mind when engineering your "free consultation" offer and subsequent process.

1. Let's be crystal clear on something: a "free consultation" is a *sales meeting*.

2. Even though it's free, a prospect still needs to be *sold* on why they need the consultation.

3. **Because it needs to be *sold*, you cannot use "free consultation" with a form below it on a web page and expect it to work.** Consultations are best "sold" either to unconverted leads who have requested information from you (because they're already engaged) or via direct mail, on webinars, at tradeshow events, or in other situations where a longer "conversation" can be had about what it is and why they need it. Quite simply, setting an appointment with you is a bigger hurdle for a prospect to jump over and therefore requires more "selling."

4. Part of "selling" the consultation is **naming it something other than a "free sales call."** That's why we call it a "free network assessment" or a "free cybersecurity risk assessment" in the IT world. Essentially, these are *all the same thing*. They are all a sales appointment—but a risk assessment appears to have more value than a free sales call, which brings me to another key point ...

5. **If you want the maximum response, a prospect *must believe they will receive value from the consultation itself even if they don't buy.*** For example, most chiropractors offer a "free X-rays and diagnostic exam" as a way of attracting new patients so you can determine where your pain is

coming from and if it can be resolved without surgery. Make no mistake, this exam *is* a sales event. They might muck it up, doing a poor job and not closing, but that doesn't change what it is. New dentists who are attempting to establish a client base will often offer a free exam and tooth whitening as a way of attracting new patients. Again, this is a *sales event* for the purpose of getting you to become a regular client. We offer a one-on-one marketing consultation that provides a prospect our Marketing Roadmap and advice on how they can double or triple the number of leads and clients they're getting—and we do that for free. All of these are examples of "free consultations" that are essentially sales events designed to get a new prospect in the door.

6. **Your marketing campaign and confirmation process should contain an explanation of "here's what will happen during/after your consultation."** People want to know what is going to happen during the consultation. Will they be embarrassed? Asked questions they don't know the answer to? Be asked to do things that will make them uncomfortable? If it's a medical consultation, will it hurt? Do they need someone to drive them? Outlining what will happen, even if it's a few lines in an email, alleviates fears they have that may prevent them from showing up to the consultation.

7. **After a lead is qualified and before the consultation happens, you should send a quality shock-and-awe box to prepare the prospect to buy.** A good one will deliver "*wow*," build trust, position *you* as a trusted advisor, overcome objections, and educate the prospect on what

"good" is (and "good" should be what you offer). Unfortunately, I don't have the ability to explain what goes into a good shock-and-awe, but we can send you an example if you call my office.

8. In most cases, you aren't going to conduct a "one-call close" with a prospect and will likely have a second or third follow-up meeting to close a contract. **Therefore, the real purpose of the *first meeting* is to *sell them on engaging in the diagnostic process itself* or taking the next step.** Now, I realize you're thinking, "Hang on a sec; if a prospect signed up for an assessment of some kind, why do I have to sell them on *doing* the assessment when I initially meet them?" In some cases, you won't—but not in 100 percent of the cases. Hence the purpose for a good quality shock-and-awe. But you also need to make sure the first call or meeting should be a verbal diagnostic process that builds trust and rapport and increases their anxiety about their situation so they are more eager to move forward. On that same thought …

9. **Your consultation *must* have a diagnostic component to it *before* you prescribe (close, propose, sell).** For example, if you called my office to inquire about working with us, and my sales rep didn't ask you *any* diagnostic questions, and didn't ask about your situation, goals, needs, budget, etc., but just started selling—*We have this toolkit. It's $5,000. Now buy it*—how quick would you be to hand the money over? I can tell you this: we would *not* have a high close ratio. If you went to a chiropractor you found online (not a referral) and he didn't do X-rays, didn't evaluate your posture, *didn't ask you any questions about your pain*, didn't ask you what you

A High-Level Overview of How We Get Prospects to Sign Up for a Consultation

- A lead opts in on a website for some type of free information and is instantly put into our CRM (Keap), and a series of emails and tasks are kicked off for follow-up. It's worth noting that while we offer multiple ways for a prospect to respond, 98 percent of our leads come in from a web form. That may be due to the fact that we're selling to IT professionals, and their preference is technology over any other form of response. Don't take that as a given for *your* clients. Currently, our best free information offers have been a webinar titled "6 Ways to Generate More Leads and Sales without Spending a Dime on Marketing" and, thanks to COVID, "The Recession Survival Guide for IT Services Businesses: How to Get Leads and Clients Spending Money on IT Services *Now*."

- The lead is immediately presented with a free one-on-one marketing consultation on the *next* page—not the information they requested. To get the free marketing consultation, they need to complete a short survey (which further qualifies the lead and provides involvement, which also helps in the sales process). If they decline, they can move on to the free information. An email is also sent automatically with a link to the free information regardless of whether or not they book the consultation.

- After they complete the survey, they are presented with a page to book their appointment. This allows over 70 percent of the consultations we get to *self-book*, which means no human was involved. So, unless you love hiring and managing sales-people, I suggest you follow my advice and allow prospects to self-book their own sales consultations.

- As soon as the lead comes in, it pops into one of our business development reps' dialers to call ASAP. They continue to make no fewer than five calls to try to book the appointment and only stop if we discover the prospect is not qualified or not interested, or they book an appointment. As the calls are made (and depending on the outcome of the call), a series of follow-up emails are also sent, driving them to book their consultation.

- Within minutes of the lead coming in, it is checked and cleaned by our database marketing administrator. She makes sure it's an MSP (or managed services provider, which is what our industry calls them), and if not, she takes a series of next steps depending on what type of lead it is, or deletes it if spam, not qualified, etc. She also uses Google search, LinkedIn, and other online tools to find out if they are the owner and to verify and update the mailing address, phone number, and email address. This is an entire process in my organization to ensure we don't add junk to our database and are able to use all media when following up. I don't have my sales reps doing this because they're often sloppy about it, and I want them spending time dialing legit prospects.

- If they are qualified, we mail them a package of informa-tion that sells the consultation and continue to email and call to follow up. Overall, this process takes about three weeks, unless, obviously, they book, say they aren't interested, or prove unqualified.

- We also kick off a retargeting campaign to follow them around the internet and on Facebook and LinkedIn to send them messages promoting the free consultation. This is currently one of the highest-performing social media campaigns we run.

- If they still don't book a consultation after all the mail, emails, calls, and retargeting, they are added to an online and offline drip marketing campaign that consists of newsletters, blog posts, and other webinars. One example of a powerful offline drip campaign is our magazine, www.MSPSuccessMagazine. com, which we send them for free.

- Every month, we pull a list of unconverted leads that have gone through the above process that are six months or older but still haven't booked or sat an appointment with one of our senior sales consultants. We clean it again, then put them through an aggressive mail/call/email campaign we call our "Godfather" offer (we make 'em an offer they can't refuse). This campaign is focused on getting them to sign up for a free consultation.

Once they book, there is also an extensive process of follow-up calls, emails, and mailing of a shock-and-awe box to ensure they actually show up for the appointment and are prepared to buy. If they sit in the consult and don't buy, we also have a follow-up campaign to try to convert them—and that list is a much hotter list that we focus on more than all other lists.

Building all of this has been a lot of work, but I can assure you it has been 100 percent, absolutely worth it. Although we continually monitor and tweak it every week, this process, the offer, and the copy have been largely untouched for years. A true marketing oil well that is still producing.

If you are an MSP, VAR, or IT services company, you can experience this for yourself by visiting www.TechnologyMarketingToolkit.com. However, if you are not an MSP, you can find out more about my private consulting services at www.RobinRobins.com. And if you're someone who would like to gain access to my IT services clients for the purpose of selling your services to them, please visit www.BigRedMedia.com for all the details.

ROBIN ROBINS is the IT industry's most in-demand marketing consultant, sales trainer, and direct-response marketing consultant who specializes in developing strategic marketing, sales, and lead-generation systems for MSPs, VARs, and IT services companies. Robin is the founder of Technology Marketing Toolkit, *MSP Success Magazine*, and Big Red Media. To date, her organization has coached, trained and consulted with over ten thousand IT business owners from all over the US and in thirty-seven different countries. She currently runs the largest C-level peer group in the IT services channel for MSPs, and her annual event, the IT Sales and Marketing Boot Camp, attracts over 1,600 attendees every year and is sponsored by the IT industry's leading vendors. Robin has been voted a number-one speaker at many industry events such as CompTIA's BreakAway, Channel Partners Conference and Expo, ASCII's boot camps, DattoCon, and IT Nation. She has been published in VAR Business, eChannelLine.com, *Sales and Marketing magazine*, Selling Power, and *SMB Partner Community magazine*. This vast experience has given Robin a broad knowledge of hundreds of marketing and sales tactics used by some of the most successful, sales-driven organizations in the world.

CHAPTER 9:

Half the Battle Won or Lost in Seventeen Words or Less

WHEN I BRIEFLY ran a relatively traditional agency and used copywriters other than myself, it was common for one of them to proudly present the draft version of an ad or a sales letter with a cute, funny, or (theoretically) clever headline that, if separated from the rest of the piece, was meaningless and had no impact. Their answer was: "If you read the copy, you'll see that the headline is brilliant." And, I always thought, if Farah Fawcett showed up at my door in that bathing suit from the wall poster, with a pizza and no desire for conversation, I'd die a happy man. But it *doesn't* work that way. *"If you read the copy, you'll see that the headline is brilliant ..."*

This is madness.

The headline or, better still, the headline "real estate"—i.e., the top one-quarter to one-third of the page of an ad (or landing page) or above the first panel of a folded sales letter—is **the ad for the ad.** It *must* sell the reader on digging into the rest of the advertising message. It is here that you win at least half the battle, securing aroused interest and thus readership.

Response comes from a *sequence of* decisions, not one decision. To respond or not to respond is not *the* question; it is *the last* question. With mail, the first is *Do I throw this out, or do I open it and look at it?* With a print ad, it is *Do I turn the page, or do I stop and read this?* I knew a fellow who often advertised a book about a certain method of getting rich with a full-page ad with no photos or pictures, dense copy requiring at least ten minutes for the average person to read it ... run in *Playboy*. On the next pages, waiting, were topless and naked young women in provocative (if wholly impractical) poses. To get readers *not* to flip the page and instead stop and read his ad was a herculean task, requiring one hell of a headline, prehead, and subhead. Wherever you advertise, you should **consider your competition for attention** urging your reader (or viewer or online visitor) to skip the ad, flip the page. And with online media, the competition for attention is fierce and ever present. There you are in a brutal death match for attention.

If you can come up with a headline that will make men tell naked women to wait while they read your ad, you've got something. That's a great headline test. Go give it to every headline of every ad, brochure, sales letter, landing page, website, etc. you now use.

(Yes, I am aware I just used two very "male" references that, in today's hypersensitive climate might be found offensive or misogynist. Should that be the case, do yourself a favor and never ask a man, What are you thinking? Oh, and ask me if I care that you found the examples too "locker room.")

How to Easily Write a Powerful Headline
(EVEN IF YOU STRUGGLE TO WRITE A GROCERY LIST)
in Fifty-Nine Minutes or Less

The good news is that what you need to craft a potent headline is the four essentials described in chapter 7. This is not the only approach to the headline, but it is a solid, reliable one: simply, **your headline should contain at least one of the four essentials, summarized**. As a big thumb rule, summarized in seventeen words or less. (I violated that limit with the above subhead, but I used a smaller font size for its middle to compensate.)

More good news: you can cheat. There are readily available fill-in-the-blank headline templates, made from already tested and proven "classics"—in my book *The Ultimate Sales Letter*; in a book by Victor Schwab, *How to Write a Good Advertisement*, and online, findable via Google. Take ten to twenty out of such sources, play with converting them to your purpose and business, and ultimately choose the two you judge best to split test or, if you must, the one you judge best to use. This is certainly doable in less than an hour.

As an example, the iconic headline "They Laughed When I Sat Down at the Piano—Until I Started to Play" converts to this fill-in-the-blank template:

They Laughed When I _____, Until I _____.

That headline was created by John Caples for a full-page ad in 1927. It has since been "swiped" and repurposed literally tens of thousands of times and is just as effective today as ever, because it leverages a commonly shared emotional experience and/or desire: after being criticized, doubted, or ridiculed for starting out to do something, succeeding at it and then "rubbing the doubters' noses in it." It could even have been used by Noah: *They Laughed When I Started Building the Ark—Until the Floods Came, and I and My Zoo Sailed Safely Away.*

CHAPTER 10:

The Three Hurdles

IN LIFE IN GENERAL, and in every individual life; in business in general, and in every individual business, there are hurdles to get over. Some people waste time on futile searches for pathways with no hurdles. Some people act as if ignoring their existence will make them go away. Smart people take inventory of theirs, then figure out how to get over them. Their success is built on reality, not fantasy. Dr. Edward Kramer wrote about this as "the positive power of *negative* preparation." More broadly, Napoleon Hill referred to it as essential "*accurate* thinking." If you want to drill down to the core of successful achievement, this is it.

To succeed, an ad must get over three hurdles:

1. Disinterest

2. Skepticism

3. Resistance

Overcoming Disinterest

Much of this can be taken care of by targeting and, with some media (like Facebook) microtargeting, so you are only presenting your ad to a select audience with a high probability of interest in it. But whether you do this or more indiscriminately place your advertising, its message must overcome

Most people start out disinterested with anything new intruding into their already busy, cluttered, difficult lives. They are never thinking about nothing. Something stands in your way, occupying the space and time you want. If your ad message *can* be ignored, *it will be.*

(1) Specific, (2) obvious, and, ideally, (3) timely or urgent relevance is the best cure for disinterest. I have a long-time client, for example, in the "money under management" business—in a very crowded, cluttered, competitive field. By "specializing" in these services for individuals soon to sell, selling, or recently having sold their companies for $20 million or more, Ted Oakley (OxbowAdvisors.com) is able to differentiate himself and do advertising that meets the above criteria: specific, obvious, and timely relevance. Instead of writing and advertising another book on investment strategies, Ted Oakley can advertise his books *$20 Million and Broke* and *Crazy Times: After the Sale.* Instead of bloviating about the same financial issues all advisors and money managers do (and must), he can write, talk, and disseminate online videos about his most popular book, *The Psychology of Staying Rich*, and he can warn of "the vultures that circle after your sale of a company."

> There is an ancient axiom about advertising and marketing: if anybody or everybody can be your customer, nobody will be.

There is an ancient axiom about advertising and marketing: if anybody or everybody can be your customer, nobody will be. You might think the odds favor being all things to all people, but this ignores the criticality of differentiation and of breaking through disinterest. **You want to be for somebody very specific, so they instantly recognize you as relevant to them.** I have termed this "message to market match." The tighter and more precise and more perfect the match is, the better the advertising will work. The sloppier and less certain and less obvious the match is, the less likely the advertising will be successful. *WHO are you for?* Is more important than *WHAT do you have to sell?* in eight or nine out of ten cases.

Overcoming Skepticism

People have it hammered into their heads:

- If it sounds too good to be true, it is.

- There *must* be a catch.

- There's no such thing as a free lunch.

People also carry around a lot of unhelpful baggage, ghosts of bad buying decisions of the past. Often, also, they are emotionally married to having "unsolvable problems" (for example, "slow metabolism") and resigned to dying with unmet desires. When you combine these attitudes, you get a high hurdle of skepticism. They don't trust "salesmen" *and* they don't trust themselves with salesmen. Gradually, once-high trust in many institutions—government, the mainstream media, academia, religious organizations, and business—has eroded, to the point of a 180-degree reversal, from the 1950s to the present. Now, no one has high trust in any of the voices trying to inform, influence, or persuade them. All things considered, skepticism is a very high hurdle.

There are many ways to counter this in advertising. Social proof is one, which is why you see testimonials used as much as they are, often referring to having had initial skepticism but ultimately loving their new whatever.

Testimonials from experts and authority figures, endorsements from celebrities, and impressive statistics ("over one million bottles sold and one million lives changed") are all tactics for overcoming skepticism.

The one thing you must *never* do is take for granted that you will be believed. Belief, even cautious hope, the opposites of skepticism, must be manufactured and made an important element of your advertising. I don't care who you are (or think you are) and why you should automatically be believed, the surer way to be successful with your advertising is to assume you won't be. Get ego and sense of entitlement out of the way!

When Lee Iacocca dragged Chrysler back from the brink of bankruptcy (the first time), he knew he had a skeptical public to face. He told me: "I thought: Who in their right mind would buy a car from a company they thought was going broke any day now? We couldn't ignore this. We had to take it on, with bold and aggressive advertising. That's why I went with the new, best warranty in the business and why I did the TV commercials personally, to stand there and promise the American public that we were for real."

Incidentally, if you will go back and reread my introduction to this book, you'll find I went to some pains to explain why I should be believed as a truth teller on this subject. If you get a copy of my book *Almost Alchemy: How to Get More from Fewer & Less*, you will find a number of impressive testimonials on the opening pages of the book. I have *not* presumed that I will be believed because of who I am, my reputation, or my authorship of a book. If I did, it would be my ego talking, my sense of entitlement at work, and it would be a grievous error.

I have written an entire book on this, the *No B.S. Trust-Based Marketing*, with a top financial advisor as my coauthor and other "high-trust sellers" as contributors.

Overcoming Resistance

Ultimately, interested people with skepticism counterweighted are *still* reluctant to place themselves into a situation where they will be sold something. Remember, it's not just that they don't trust salespeople; *they don't trust themselves with salespeople.* As I noted above, ghosts of all their past bad buying decisions, disappointments, and humiliations haunt them.

If your advertising is tasked with bringing a prospective customer, client, patient, or donor into an in-person, face-to-face, telephone, or even online situation where he will "be sold," it must tactically address and try to allay that prospect's reluctance to put himself in such a situation. You will sometimes see this done with message copy about no pressure, no obligation, free trial, etc. Sometimes with message copy about value from the appointment (exam, meeting, call, etc.) itself—like my copy device: "7 Questions That Will Be Answered by Your 29-Minute Free Exam."[7] Sometimes by outright bribery, like a

---

7   I first created this copy device for the chiropractic profession in the early 1980s and have since deployed it in healthcare re exams for hearing aids and dental and orthodontic practices, as well as in advertising for over twenty-five thousand offices; in financial services re free seminars and in-office appointments, for thousands of advisors; and in numerous other categories of business.

$50 Dine-Out or Amazon gift card with your free estimate, whether you then get the product or service or not.

Really exceptional advertising or follow-up to lead generation advertising can *also* reduce resistance to buying when that moment of decision comes. But *at minimum*, your advertising must acknowledge and assuage peoples' resistance to risking being sold to. A worthy goal is "*zero*-resistance selling," about which I wrote a book by that title. Through the bridge you build between a person's first, tentative expression of interest to point of sale, you can reduce or even erase *their* resistance. This bridge's components may include establishing authority (thus the power to prescribe rather than sell), demonstrating reliability (by on time, complete follow-up), presentation of social proof, and persuading of both scarcity and urgency. You can reduce or erase your or your salesperson's *inner* resistance with the knowledge that your advertising was engineered to attract appropriate prospects (with ability and willingness to buy) and your presales appointment bridge is well built and fully utilized. However, before this opportunity occurs, your advertising has to ease resistance to just responding to advertising in the first place.

If your advertising contains the four essentials (chapter 7) and overcomes these three hurdles, it has a high, high probability of success.

CHAPTER 11:

What's Your Big Idea? (What It *Isn't*)

ALMOST ALL GREAT ad campaigns have, as a beating heart, a Big Idea screaming to get out. It is news. It differentiates with competitive advantage. It has promise of benefit. And it is *big*. *BIG!*

One of the best of Donald Trump's Trumpian quotes, lived by throughout his career, is "If you are going to bother to think at all, why not think big?" With this as a governing principle, he left "small real estate" in Queens and invaded Manhattan, where he literally changed the city's skyline. His longtime right-hand dealmaker, George Ross, says Trump never bought a building to remake or started a building, hotel, golf club, etc. without a Big Idea for it to advertise itself with. Most recently, of course, Trump defied all political convention, mounted a hostile takeover of the Republican Party, and ran for and won the presidency of the United States without ever holding any elected office—largely on the strength of three Big Ideas. Whatever happens going forward, to this point he has been the personification of the power of the Big Idea.

A classic in success literature is David Schwartz's *The Magic of Thinking Big*. I have probably read it fifty times, starting at around age sixteen.

All exceptional, exceptionally successful businesses have/ create their own Big Ideas. Bezos made Amazon into "The Everything Store"; they created their own substitute for "Black Friday" that everybody else competes in, with Amazon Prime Day(s). Dominos skyrocketed originally with "Delivered in 30 Minutes or Less, Guaranteed," now antiquated because everybody caught up, but then a Very Big Idea. The Sandals resorts led with "all-inclusive," mimicking cruise ships' formats on dry land. Pay attention: you will notice the use of or absence of the Big Idea everywhere.

> The Big Idea is what the product isn't. What it doesn't require. What is omitted from it.

How do *you* get one of these Big Ideas?

There are a number of paths, and those of us who devise ad campaigns for a living use them all. Here, I'll give you one well-traveled path. Once you have it explained, you'll spot it in one ad campaign after another (particularly those that can be trusted as "great" because they are run by direct-response companies a lot for months or years). The Big Idea is what the product *isn't*. What it *doesn't* require. What is *omitted* from it.

First, some golden oldies: Robert Allen coined the term and popularized the concept of **"*Nothing Down* Real Estate."** At the time, when a 20 percent down payment on a mortgage was the norm, it was a radical promise: that you could be a successful real estate investor with *no* capital and even *no* credit and buy properties with *nothing down*. Promoted by Bob and an army of copycats, this Big Idea packed hotel ballrooms with thousands of "students" coast to coast every weekend, and virtually birthed an industry. It popularized a previously obscure business, largely credited to a man named Al Lowry. It made full-page newspaper ads, magazine ads, direct mail, radio ads, TV commercials, and TV infomercials work. Bob's prime years with this predated the internet or he'd have dominated online media with this as well. Today's promoters of the same type of real estate investing successfully use every online media. Many even get their own "reality TV shows" on cable stations. I have had several of these modern leaders of this field as clients, like Ron LeGrand, and I have helped others do start-ups. They have all relied on, in large part, the Big Idea first made mainstream by Robert Allen.

As I write this, I'm working with a client, Dr. David Phelps, who provides coaching and resources exclusively to affluent dentists within ten years of anticipated exit from practice on real estate investing (FreedomFounders.com). His Big Idea is "For dentists ready to ditch Wall Street and take control of their retirement … create wealth and freedom *without Wall Street*."

Another great opportunity Big Idea was "How to Get A Second Paycheck—without a Second Job."

"Does She or Doesn't She?" was a deliberately provocative Big Idea for its time, using sexual innuendo to grab attention, to then advertise Clairol's at-home hair dye kits. At the time, if women colored their hair, it was supposed to be a secret, and it was done at a salon. Talking about it out in the open was daring, and overcoming skepticism about doing it yourself at home and *omitting* the beauty parlor was a high hurdle. The Big Idea that followed this was

"Blondes Have More Fun—Why Shouldn't *You* Live Your Life as a Blonde?"

Another beauty category Big Idea that I did advertising and marketing for was "The *Non*-Surgical, At-Home Facelift—Look 10 Years Younger in Just 29 Minutes."

A more contemporary Big Idea ad campaign example is Nutri-System's premade weight-loss meals, advertised emphasizing that there's *no* calorie or carb counting, *no* meetings and weigh-ins, *no* this or that; **"*just* eat the food, lose the weight."** Subtraction, not addition.

Sometimes a product's features can contain the Big Idea needed for successful ad campaigns, like Sleep Number Beds—initially sneered at by the industry as nothing more than a gimmick, or *self-parking* cars. But more often, more reliably the Big Idea is waiting in what the product isn't, doesn't require, or eliminates.

One way or another, the Big Idea *needs* to be found or imagined and manufactured. Don't leave home without it!

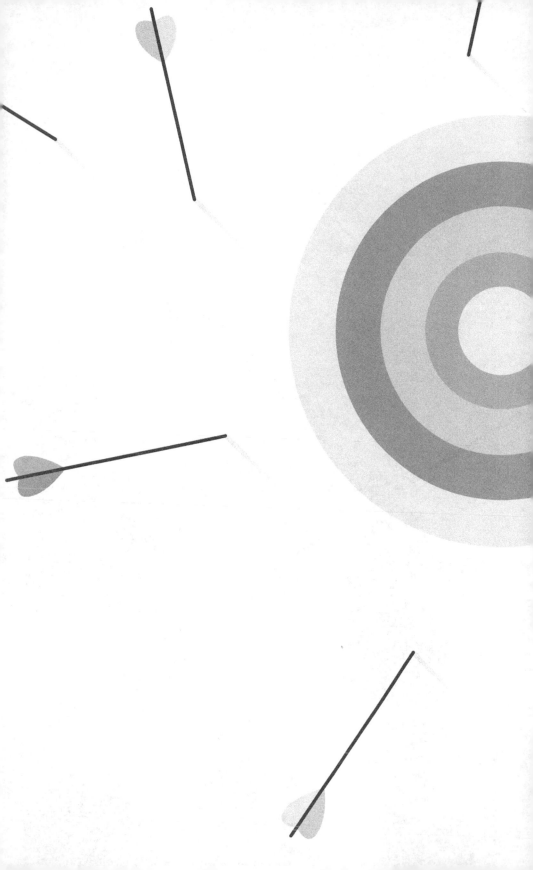

12

Failure to Test

YOU HAVE TO be careful with assumption. "Assume" can make an Ass out of U and Me! **Success with advertising is not often made from what you *think*. It comes from what you *know*. Facts matter; opinions don't,** and this includes yours, your staff's, your mother-in-law's, your "expert" web developer's, and your ad agency's. Facts matter; opinions do not. This is "tough stuff." People routinely act as if opinions and facts are one and the same, when, *in fact*, they are as different as horses and zebras. Everybody is entitled to their opinions, educated and expert or not, but nobody is entitled to their own facts. To be successful in general and especially with advertising, you need a healthy respect for facts and a healthy skepticism toward opinions.

Getting to the facts that can then produce a successful ad is often only possible by somehow testing and split testing alternatives and alternate options of elements within an ad or its equivalents, like landing pages at web sites.

Asked how he made his greatest discoveries, Einstein said, "I grope." He might have been an Ad Man.

Surprises from Tests

The now-famous author Tim Ferriss reportedly found the title for his first bestselling book *The 4-Hour Workweek* by split testing a hundred possible titles with small ads on Google AdWords. It was ***not* his** top pick. He wisely let the market pick his bet for him.

I am a world-class copywriter, and I *know* what comprises a great title, headline, ad theme, ad narrative—but that does *not* mean I know which of a number of options, all containing the right elements, will resonate best with a particular intended audience at a particular point in time. I don't, and nobody else does either. In picking winners in advance of testing, I've been right more often than not, but there have still often been instances where my top pick was just the third runner up, and the winner by far was one I wrote but *not* one I liked best. I confess this. Most copywriters won't. They prefer you believing they have psychic ability.

Look Closely: One *Letter* = A Million-Dollar Difference

One of the all-time classic examples of why you test, from the annals of advertising, is an accidental split-test against this headline: "Put Music in Your Life."

By accident one week the ad was running, a newspaper's typographer incorrectly added an *s* to *put*, making the headline "Puts Music in Your Life," which out-pulled the original by a multiple. With 20/20 hindsight,

> The internet has made split testing almost ridiculously easy, yet many advertisers do not take advantage of the opportunities

it is obvious why: *put* requires action and effort on your part and allows doubts about whether you can or will do the work; *puts* promises to do it for you. Tougher to see this with foresight than with hindsight.

The internet has made split testing almost ridiculously easy, yet many advertisers do not take advantage of the opportunities as Tim Ferriss did. One of the most brilliant "test and split test everything gurus" helping people use all the online media and opportunities today is Russell Brunson, and I suggest looking him up online and looking in on his work and his resources.

There *are* shortcuts. Assembling advertising from what you *know* works can greatly reduce the testing and split testing needed to arrive at a winner. Chief sources of what is *known* to work are:

SHORTCUT #1: SALES SCRIPTS

What you or your top salespeople say to prospects, transcribed if not already in written script form, can "migrate" to ad media. I routinely commanded six-figure fees as an ad copywriter, but I never assumed I knew more than the person going nose to nose, toes to toes with prospects everyday actually selling the product or service to be advertised. I always wanted transcripts of recordings of the client or his top salespeople in my raw material stack.

SHORTCUT #2: SWIPE FILES AND LEGAL THEFT

Most ads, direct-mail pieces, websites, etc. are copyright protected, so outright plagiarism is illegal as well as immoral. However, extracting parts 'n' pieces from successful models and creatively adapting them *is* legal, ethical, and smart. The caution is that you are borrowing from *successful* examples. It's hard to trust any but those soliciting direct and immediate response, thus likely to be tracked and held accountable by their owners.

Over time, you should build up your own "swipe file" of ads, direct-mail pieces, downloaded web content, and other examples of advertising you have reason to believe is successfully generating response and sales from the very same prospects you want to influence, in your business or product category, but also in others. The My Pillow commercials' messages are not just relevant to pillow merchants, but also to mattress retailers and chiropractors.

SHORTCUT #3: DIRECT CONVERSATIONS, INTERVIEWS, AND IN-THE-TRENCHES EXPERIENCE

Nothing beats going into the woods where your target customers live, work, and recreate. If you are selling to low- to middle-income families and you don't often hang out at a Walmart, watch, eavesdrop, and engage people in conversation, you are a fool. If you sell to rich folk who own yachts and you aren't at the big boat show from its opening to its close, doing the same thing, you are a fool.

This is tied to a big, big secret of advertising failure versus advertising success. This is 24 karat gold. You might want to write it down. Most advertising that fails is *product centric*. Most advertising that succeeds is *people centric*.

People are *not*, by and large, all that interested in products or services and their features and benefits, and they are definitely not as interested in *your* product or service as (A) you are, and (B) as you think they should be. People *are* interested mostly in themselves. The things they think about most, are most amenable to talking about, and tie their buying behavior to can be remembered as **FORM**:

F amily

O ccupation

R ecreation

M oney

A product that *nobody* is interested in talking about—life and disability insurance or annuities—has to be advertised and then sold by talking about FORM.

FAMILY

- If something happens to you, what will happen to them?

- As a responsible family leader ...

OCCUPATION

- You take pride in putting a roof over their heads, in putting food on the table, in the harvest from your hard work ...

- As a (dentist, lawyer, etc.) you are painfully aware your income is 100 percent dependent on your ability to work ...

RECREATION

- The freedom to enjoy your "thing" (golf, fishing, etc.) is important to you—did you know you can *guarantee* that for life?

MONEY

- There is a big difference between retiring and retiring well ...

- Did you know you can *insure income*—against your own illness, injury, or inability to work?

If you are interested in a much more sophisticated understanding of how to talk to people about themselves for purpose of fast rapport and successful persuasion, the most powerful tactics are in what fortune tellers and psychics have relied on for centuries and still do today: the "cold read." A great education in this, including word-for-word scripts, can be found in the book *The Full Facts Book of Cold Reading* by Ian Rowland. There are other books on the subject as well, so an Amazon or Google search of "cold reading" will offer choices.

SHORTCUT #4: PEER AND MASTERMIND REVIEWS AND FOCUS GROUPS

Michael Masterson is not only an expert copywriter and ad copy chief; he may have developed more top copywriters "from scratch" than any living human. Mike Palmer is one of the most successful direct-response copywriters. Together, they have a *peer group process* for turning out top-performing copy even if initiated by "B" and "C" level copywriters. Together they wrote the book *Copy Logic: The New Science of Producing Breakthrough Copy (without Criticism).* I think it's a poorly titled book that deserves much better, because it lays out in transparent detail exactly how their process is used, within one of the largest and most successful direct-marketing companies and by freelancers. If you feel the need for creative, constructive support for your own advertising, written by you or for you by others, this book is the elegantly simple set of instructions.

I was social distancing before social distancing was cool! While I am personally a loner and a hermit and have great trust in my own copywriting, there are still times that I assemble and use different kinds of "focus groups" or "peer review groups." As example, I have, on three different occasions, written a "bank" of ad copy about the number-one OTC acne product, ProActiv®, for a long-, longtime client, the Guthy-Renker Corporation. Absent preteens and teens underfoot, I recruited paid readers—moms and dads of preteens and teens, and their kids—to read and comment on my ad copy, especially to note where it "didn't ring right." I chose parent-readers who had some experience, current work, or at least great interest in copywriting, recruited from the ranks of members of American Writers & Artists.[8] Money well spent.

If you are part of a professionally run Mastermind Group, you will have excellent opportunities to get knowledgeable peer input about your advertising (as well as all your business principles, strategies, and tactics). Caveat: listen, consider, weigh input, but never set aside your own knowledge or gut instincts without testing.

If you are unfamiliar with the Mastermind Concept, it dates at least to the industrial revolution, with men like Carnegie, Ford, Firestone, and Edison, as described in detail by Napoleon Hill in his books *Laws of Success* and *Think and Grow Rich*. In part, the concept is that several minds joined together in like-minded harmony and common purpose create an *extra supermind* with powers far beyond that of mere mortals. From a less metaphysical standpoint, it is at least true that the given mastermind group's participants benefit from the combined experience, information, and contacts of all, an obvious force multiplier.

SHORTCUT #5: USE OF PROFESSIONAL COPYWRITERS

In many situations where small businesses advertise, the owner can't afford top pro copywriters and blessedly may not need them; the

---

8   American Writers & Artists is an organization of freelance copywriters and writers, as well as an educational resource for them. They maintain a "jobs board," where clients can advertise to find appropriate writers, and directories for writers. Several self-study courses that I've produced for copywriters are housed there: www.awaionline.com.

level of competitors' capability and the effectiveness of their advertising will be so low, you can outperform doing your own advertising copywriting yourself. It is a version of the old joke about the advisability of taking a fat, slow buddy along on hikes deep into a forest—should a hungry bear appear, you need not outrun the bear; you just need to outrun the fat guy. Also, there are "template" and "fill in the blank" resources available inexpensively for the copywriting do-it-yourselfer, such as my book *The Ultimate Sales Letter* and *The Magnetic Marketing System*®, the former available at Amazon, the latter at magneticmarketingstore.com.

When the size and scope of your opportunities justifies it, the use of one or several professional, freelance copywriters can be a potent shortcut to successful results, because their cumulative experience and specialized knowledge is brought to bear on your project. I, for example, have written ad copy for clients for some forty years, retaining 85 percent of clients over time, with fees that went from an average of $5,000 per project to $100,000 plus royalties per project, and over half that work concentrated in just four categories of products and businesses: information marketing (i.e., publishing, membership, seminars and conferences, coaching); self-improvement and success education; skin care, cosmetics, diet, and weight loss; and financial services and investments. If yours is one of those three, then you benefit from *all* the work I've done before yours, which has eliminated a lot of experimentation, even to the point of making success for you a déjà vu all over again for me. But no "A-level" copywriter is a cheap date, so the opportunity must be appropriate.

There are "A-," "B-," and "C-level" copywriters, and different businesses have different needs at different times, so a "C" may be adequate and affordable for one ad project while only an "A" will do for another. Big direct marketing firms tend to use all three capability levels of copywriters, and may have in-house, salaried writers and use outside freelancers as well. A good place to learn about and shop for freelancers is at awaionline.com (American Writers and Artists). If you are part of a good mastermind/coaching group, members will have different experiences with different copywriters, and can share that information.

The Copywriter Behind the Curtain

Words matter. *A* **word can matter.** During the prime months of COVID-19, "*sanitized*" suddenly became an important word in advertising for all sorts of products, services, and businesses—auto service departments at dealerships, carpet cleaning, high-pressure cleaning of home exteriors, even pizza delivery boxes. Clorox rushed new cleaning "and sanitizing" products and product labels to market. **Whose voice words are in matters**. With Victoria Principal Skin Care products sold by TV infomercials, having her deliver the "bottom of the jar guarantee" first person, from her, rather than from the company, by a nameless, faceless voice-over had a significant impact on sales, a choice I championed. These are the kind of decisions that experienced, skilled copywriters can make, that make a difference.

> You should never underestimate or discount the importance of the copy and copywriting.

You should *never* **underestimate or discount the importance of the copy and copywriting**. It is usually more important than the product or service itself, often able to create fortunes from relatively mundane, common, and competition-burdened products.

My copy (and copy written by others) had more to do with Proactiv® becoming a billion-dollar brand and enterprise than did the "glop" itself. My copy put over two hundred thousand people a year into a particular personal finance–related seminar; the seminar itself didn't do that; the copy in the direct-mail pieces did. My copy *was* the start-up of highly successful, multimillion-dollar, specialized training organizations in the restaurant, menswear retail, chiropractic, dental, legal, and other niches. It *all* started with a print ad for a trade journal and a sales letter for the mail, all living or dying by the copy. Countless businesses you know as giants today owe their birth and existence to a copywriter! We may be "invisible." We don't get author credits like book authors. We work behind the curtain. But that doesn't mean we aren't vital.

As analogy, consider the magic performed by the most famous professional magicians, past and present, from Houdini and Thurston to Copperfield and Penn & Teller. Behind the curtain, each has at least one "supermechanic" who turns their ideas for a "new" illusion into engineering, into a manufactured and tested "trick." As another analogy, when you watch an action movie full of death-defying car chases and crashes, heroes surviving explosions, and violent fight scenes occurring in incredible locations, you see the actors and/or their stunt doubles on the screen, but behind the curtain, a seasoned professional stunt coordinator and his engineers made the stunt work. Hal Needham, for example, invented a hidden spring-loaded platform that literally rocket-launches a stunt man as an explosion occurs, getting him far enough away, fast enough to avoid serious injury. What goes on behind the curtain in most successes is typically much more important than what is seen in front of it.

Having said that, it's important to remember that you can delegate to and/or obtain input from professional copywriters, but you should *never abdicate* to them. Their role is to interpret what you *know* about your customers, your competitive environment, and your product into a magnetic, persuasive message.

Let's be clear: *none* of these pretest shortcuts are definitively predictive, only indicative. They each have inherent flaws, so they can*not* be relied on, but they can be considered, can be helpful, can cut costs of experimentation. But they are *not* insurance. There is *no* "certainty insurance" for advertising. There is rarely a simple, straight line to successful advertising (or, for that matter, successful anything else; instead there is, as *Psycho-Cybernetics'* author Dr. Maxwell Maltz described it, "zig-zag" and "course corrections." This is good news for you if you are methodical and persistent, because most people, including your competitors, are not!

Are You Any Smarter Today about Your Business Than You Were Yesterday?

You don't get richer without getting smarter. Make a note.

In 2016, Brad Pasquale, then Donald Trump's digital advertising and social media wizard, ran *5.9 million* **separate, different ads on Facebook** and other social media platforms. In them, he conducted **hundreds of thousands of split tests**. The collected data and intelligence about what worked with different microtargeted audiences was then migrated into notes for Trump about which of his key points and promises to emphasize at a rally in one city versus different ones to emphasize at a rally in a different city; into fundraising campaigns; and into direct mail.

In comparison, the Hillary Clinton campaign ran 66,000 such ads. **Trump *5.9 million*. Hillary 66,000**. But it isn't just the dramatic difference in sheer quantity; it's the information gleaned from daily, even hourly tests, and the smart use of it.

Pasquale built a database of more than 200 million Trump-leaning voters, with their mobile phone numbers obtained by various means—and sent over *one billion text messages* to them in the months before the election. This effort also involved a large number of message tests and split tests.

As I'm writing this, the 2020 election has just ended, almost, with some legal skirmishing still underway. The new plague and its destruction or "pause" of much of the US economy was one "wild card" of several thrown into the game. Trump was also blocked from using some of the same tactics on Facebook, and midway through the campaign he also lost Pasquale. Thus, the 2020 outcome does *not* reflect badly on the brilliance of Pasquale's work in 2016. Its point remains: *applied* knowledge is power. *Testing and split testing* yield practicable knowledge.

Years back, I did a fair amount of consulting and copywriting work for Weight Watchers. At the time, their phone rooms were fielding about one million inbound calls per year, most bought with advertising. One of the first things I did was park myself in one of the phone centers in Long Island, New York, put on headphones and listen to the live calls, moving from one rep to the next for an entire day. I was horrified by much of what I heard, but most horrified by the fact that, with all that quantity of opportunity, *nothing* was being split tested! Not the script, not offers, not bonus gifts with kept appointment, not upsells, not anything. Thus—and this is important—**at the end of the day *nobody* was any smarter about the business than they were at the start**. Not the telemarketers, not the advertising people, not the CEO, nobody. This place was more comparable to a state prison with inmates just putting in time than to a dynamic marketing laboratory where discoveries were being made and results scientifically improved.

The question I urge my clients to ask themselves every night, between dinner with the family and bedtime prayers is: *What do you know now relevant to your business that you didn't know at breakfast?* If you don't have a good answer, you have failed at one of your important responsibilities. You don't get richer without getting smarter. *Self*-improvement leads income improvement.

13

CHAPTER 13:

Advertising Is *Not* (Just) Something You *Do*

LOOK OUT—HERE COMES some pretty advanced, sophisticated stuff!

My career has been much about creating **advertising** *assets*, not just doing advertising. Most business owners spend on advertising, but the really smart ones *invest* in developing advertising assets.

The watchword here is **"evergreen."** An ad, direct-mail piece, webinar, etc. is "evergreen" if it has a very long life and can be productively used on a continuous or, at least, a seasonal or rotational basis. Ideally, it can be "set it and forget it."

We have a long-time Member, an orthodontist who *owns* a seasonal four-step direct-mail campaign created in 2010 and used profitably every year since, and a radio ad that has aired on a regular, "set it and forget it" schedule for the past four years. These are perfect examples of advertising assets. These "do" for him. He doesn't do them.

There is a tendency to keep creating new advertising. I had a client for whom I had created a thirty-minute TV infomercial that ran continuously and profitably for nine years. It still holds the record for longest-running pure lead-generation infomercial. During those years one of my most vital jobs was frequently talking him out of producing a new one to replace the winner *he* was weary of watching!

Early in my speaking career, a legendary wise elder told me: *It is easier to get a new audience than it is to get a new speech that works.* I came to realize he was 1000 percent right, and I soon developed a single speech I gave word for word forty

> No ad is "old" to the person giving it their attention for the first time.

to seventy times a year, generating seven figures in sales every year for my product The Magnetic Marketing System®. The speech was, in reality, an ad, and developing a top-performing ad is a lot harder than constantly bringing new eyeballs to it. **No ad is "old" to the person giving it their attention for the first time**. Once you have a winner, you want to concentrate on driving people to it—not shelving it and working on a new replacement for it.

It is damnably hard to convince business owners of this, and to keep them on the straight and narrow, which is (1) focus your every effort on getting ownership of an evergreen advertising asset—plus (2) deploy that asset every way, in every media possible, as much as possible.

My colleague Craig Simpson,[9] a mailing list "guru" and freelance direct-mail project manager, has made millions for a longtime client by taking that client's successful TV ads for diets, skin care products,

---

9   Craig Simpson is a bona fide, trustworthy expert on direct mail, and specifically on analysis, selection, and procurement of mailing lists. His book *The Direct-Mail Solution* is a primer. Other information from Craig is available at simpson-direct.com.

fitness gadgets, etc. and converting them to direct-mail packages. Often, the TV campaign wears out long before the direct mail does. I have used this same strategy for several clients, also

Innovate and implement more; invent less.

with great success. For one of my businesses, I converted a speech to a long, multipage sales letter nearly verbatim and mailed it profitably every month for several years. In short, what works in any media will often work in many media. And it is easier to get new audiences to a winning ad than to create another winning ad.

This fits with a broader success principle from my Renegade Millionaire System, for all entrepreneurial activity: **innovate and implement more; invent less.**

Contrary to legend, Thomas Edison was a much better promoter than he was inventor. In fact, everything he is widely credited with inventing had been invented before by somebody else. Jeff Bezos invented nothing when birthing or building Amazon. Invention can, *occasionally*, produce fame and fortune, but the much, much, much more certain pathway is by innovation or adaptation of what has already been invented, then dogged implementation of a marketing system for it.

Most entrepreneurs are *emotionally* drawn to the opposite behavior. They are easily bored with dogged implementation and magnification of what works, and easily seduced and interested by "new ideas" and invention. As always, the behavior of the majority is "wrong" about moneymaking.

Walt Kelly's great cartoon character Pogo once returned from a search of an encampment's perimeter with this report: "We have met the enemy and He is Us." We *can* be our own worst enemy. We have to be smart enough and disciplined enough to recognize when our preferred behavior is not in our overall best interests.

Can *One* Great Ad Make You Rich?

Yes. Absolutely. For clients, I have created over one hundred different ads, sales letters, TV infomercials, webinars, and other ad media items, each producing over $1 million, some ten or twenty times that, and in a few cases even more. Many of these have worked for their owners for three, five, seven, ten, even fifteen years with few if any changes. Any one of these, used wisely and with every opportunity, could make you rich if you owned it.

This all starts with intention and purpose, and an understanding of wealth versus income. As a backseat driver, I can suggest that a better title for Napoleon Hill's classic *Think and Grow Rich* would have been: *Think* Differently *and Grow Rich*.

There are basically three means of producing or attracting money:

1. Work

2. People (Work Multiplied)

3. Money Put to Work (Investment and Leverage)

The first two create *income*. Only the third builds *wealth*. Therefore, it is *vital to train and discipline yourself to think like an investor*, not (just) a worker—and to think like an investor about *everything*, including advertising. When you do, your intention and objective will shift from doing advertising that will stir up some sales to building and owning evergreen advertising assets that will work for you consistently, in multiple media, over an extended period of time. With this, you will be thinking very differently than 99 percent of advertisers about advertising.

This begs another warning about delegating too much to agencies and being influenced too much by agencies, of any sort: *they* need you to constantly need, want, and pay to replace "old" with "new," to create new ad campaigns and new media constantly. This is inherent conflict of interest, if you are thinking like an investor and your interest is owning evergreen advertising assets. This does not mean you can't or shouldn't use various kinds of media agencies and vendors, but it puts the responsibility on you to be clear *and stubborn* about your intentions and to direct their work being done for you.

WWWS: What Would Warren Say?

Warren Buffet suggests an excellent question for amateur investors: *If you could only invest in five stocks in your entire life, would the one you are about to buy be one of them?* As an investor in advertising for your business, you can consider a similar question: *If you could only invest in and own five ad campaigns your entire time in your business, would this be one of them? (Can it be that "evergreen"?)*

Let's be very clear, and let's simplify how money works: you get income from what you do. You get *wealth* from what you *own*. You probably wouldn't want to invest in an apartment building that had to be blown up and torn down every four months and replaced with a new one. It would still produce some rental income, but it would never produce wealth. If somebody tried pitching you on that proposition, you'd laugh them out of the room. You'd recognize it was a great deal for the construction company, but a lousy deal for you. Think of your advertising the same way. *If it isn't going to be "built to last," should you invest in building it at all?*

People who sell you advertising and media, especially the newest fads "you have to do because everybody is doing them," *hate* this apartment building investment analogy. Yet its logic is unassailable.

I would also make the point that you might not want to build your apartment building on a known earthquake fault line or on a steep hillside known for annual mudslides, where the very earth can be yanked out from under you. Google, YouTube, Facebook, and Twitter are such places, where businesses live in constant peril. The facts about this are also unassailable. I can't tell you not to use these media if they are accessible to you and productive for you, but I can urge you *not* to make them the foundation of your entire business, its marketing, customer acquisition, or customer retention. Doing so is flat-out foolish.

CHAPTER 14:

Maximizing Every Ad Dollar You Spend, Creating Funnels That Guide EVERY Lead to Become Your Next Lifetime Customer, Client, Patient, or Member

by Russell Brunson, cofounder, ClickFunnels.com

I'VE BEEN COLLECTING junk mail since the age of twelve. I'd watch TV or listen to the radio, waiting for the commercials, because to me marketing and sales were the real entertainment. I've been a student of Dan Kennedy and Bill Glazer for over twenty years, and I'm pumped to share with you *THE single biggest opportunity to GUARANTEE that your advertising will never fail you again*!

As a youngster I'd opt in to every business opportunity offer that I could find, simply to study the art and science of direct response.

In high school I was a state champion wrestler and then became All-American in my senior year, taking second place in the country at high school nationals. I continued to wrestle in college, learning valuable lessons about competition, hard work, and the art of winning, and I graduated as one of the top ten wrestlers nationally.

In 2003, I had my first success as an online marketer selling a software called ZipBrander. ZipBrander was a viral marketing tool that not only drove laser-targeted traffic to your website but helped increase back-end profits automatically.

Two years later, in 2005, I created another product that I eventually became famous for: *How to Create a Potato Gun* DVDs. This was a simple instructional course where buyers had an option to purchase my potato gun kit (which included all the needed supplies) as an upsell. These initial products launched me into the world of internet marketing, where I quickly became one of the top marketing minds in the world.

Within a year of graduating college, I had made my first million dollars selling products. I'm not sharing this to brag but rather to open your eyes up to the great opportunity that I'll be sharing with you in this chapter.

I sold everything from shakes and supplements, to coaching, books, consulting, coupons, T-shirts, technology services, and software. I even reached top-ranking status in several network marketing companies, winning a Ferrari and *generating 1.5 million leads in just six weeks!*

Eventually, the limitations and obstacles I encountered with the technology required to bring my lead generation and sales funnels to life became the birthplace of the idea for my software company, ClickFunnels. Together with my partner, Todd Dickerson, we launched ClickFunnels in October 2014, and the company grew to $100,000,000 in the first three years.

Currently, we have over a hundred thousand active users, and I'd like to share with you THE one big secret that I have learned watching data from our users and our own funnels: **95 percent of my revenue comes from just three basic funnels...**

I know, it's fun to talk about all of the strategies and variations and cool things we can do with sales and marketing funnels. In fact, over the past few months, there have been dozens of products created on funnel strategy, and even I talk a lot about them on my podcasts, my blog, Instagram, Facebook, and in my books.

But when I started to look closely at where the majority of my income comes from, it's almost all from just three very specific funnels.

The Funnel Fundamentals

When I was a wrestler in high school, every summer we would go to wrestling camps and learn "wrestling camp" moves. You know, the fun moves, the throws and the tricks that are fun to show off to your friends and make you feel like you learned a lot. But when you look at the state, national, and world tournaments, almost every match consists of just two or three moves—single legs, double legs ... the fundamentals.

A few years later, when I started teaching wrestling camps, just like everyone else, instead of focusing on teaching the fundamentals, I started to teach "wrestling camp" moves. Why? Because they are fun to talk about, and people get so excited when they see them.

Unfortunately, the fundamentals are rarely as exciting, yet _the fundamentals are what actually win matches_.

The same is true with your online sales funnels. The more you focus on the fundamentals and ignore the flash, the more money you'll make.

I review tons of funnels, and I see people who have thousands of variations based on every scenario they can think of—upsells, down sales, cross sales, crazy email sequences, and more—yet most of them are making no money.

So I wanted to quickly share with you how you can convert your advertising dollars to cash flow and new customers!

I'm not going to give you a million ideas of cool things you "could" do but instead give you the only three things that you have to do to have success. Many gurus prefer to keep you in perpetual confusion and chasing the "next thing."

I hope that what you lose in flashy excitement, you'll make up for in increased clarity, focus, and cash flow in your company.

But please don't dismiss the simplicity of these fundamentals.

They are where you should be focusing if you want to grow in your company.

I'm going to show you behind the scenes of my three core funnels. I'm 100 percent aware that your company is probably a little different than mine.

Whenever I share these in public, there are always a few people who come up to me afterward to explain to me why their company can't use any of the three funnels.

"But I'm a financial planner, so I can't use these..." or "I'm a dentist, and none of these make sense for my practice."

What? Are you serious? Come on, guys. It just takes a little creativity to use any of these funnels in your company.

The three funnels that generate 95 percent of my revenue are...

1. The "Tripwire Funnel," where we'll begin the conversion process

2. The "Webinar Funnel," where we begin to warm up our leads and begin to bring them into our community

3. The "High-Ticket Funnel"

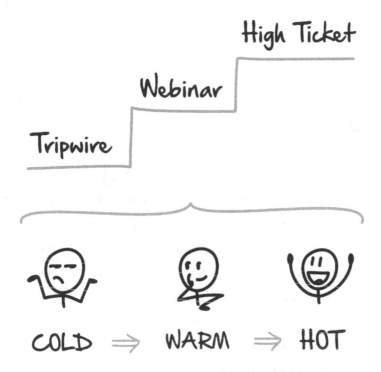

How the Three Funnels Work Together

In a perfect world, I would only offer my best result to my potential customers.

The problem is that usually my best thing is going to cost a lot of money. In my company we sell $100,000 packages, but if I were to walk up to most people on the road and say something like, "Hey, my name is Russell Brunson. I know I look like I'm twelve years old, but I'm actually really good at marketing and business, and if you give me $100,000, I'll change your business forever."

What do you think they would say?

Yeah, if they didn't laugh themselves to death, then they'd probably call the cops. Why?

Because I haven't provided any value to them yet. They have no frame of reference if I'm any good at what I do and if I really can overdeliver for them.

But if they do receive value from me first (usually on a lower-ticket product that they don't have as big of a risk to try out), then they will naturally want more.

For example, earlier this year, I sold a copy of my book *DotCom Secrets* to a guy named Tim Schmidt who owns the United State Concealed Carry Association (USCCA). He read the book, received value from it, and then called our office and within a week had sent me $100,000 to help his team implement the concepts from the book!

Because he had received value from my book, he knew I could deliver exactly what his company needed help with.

While most of the people who purchase my book don't end up giving me $100,000 that fast (unfortunately), those who do receive value from it usually will start and continue buying things from me from that point forward (unless I do something to hurt the relationship).

That is the key with everything you sell, to offer a product and an experience that will give people so much value they will want to keep coming for more.

Any time I start a new company, I always try to identify a value ladder that I want my customers to ascend.

And as I was looking closer at the value ladders we've created in our companies, all of them ascend people up the value ladder through three funnels!

Yes, the same three funnels I talked about earlier!

Let me show you what it looks like.

Core Funnel #1: Tripwire Funnel

This is the first of the three core funnels.

Typically it's some type of "free plus shipping" offer focused on cold traffic (people who don't know who you are). Perry Belcher nicknamed these types of funnels "tripwires," and the name has stuck.

I've used tripwire offers that were free books, free CDs, DVDs, MP3 players, scripts, and more.

The key to a good tripwire offer is to first think about who your dream clients are.

What would they want?

What would get them to stop in their tracks, raise their hands, and let you know that they are your dream customers?

If you can figure out what that bait is, then you'll have a successful tripwire funnel.

Dan teaches us as smart direct response marketers **we make a sale to get a customer**, we don't make a sale to make a sale.

Read that a second time.

The goal of making a sale is to acquire an ideal customer that will become a lifetime customer, client, or patient worth 10x, 100x, or more of the first sale over their lifetime.

The single goal of a "tripwire" offer is to create a customer. In all of your advertising you want to create special offers that could include some low-dollar offer that's relevant to the solution that your prospect is looking for, or it can be FREE information that your ideal customers, clients, and patients are attracted to.

THE SECRET FORMULA

Who?   Where?   BAIT?   Result?

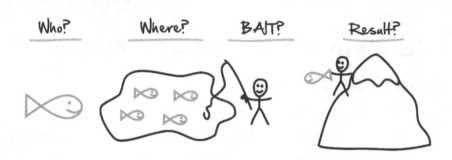

Once you get the ideal customer to raise their hand, you then begin to "indoctrinate" them to your business and your community through follow-up to help lead them to your next step.

Between the time that someone actually requests your FREE information and takes advantage of your low-dollar offer, there are about ten million distractions that could keep them from taking the next step.

If you're not careful, the people you paid to raise their hands for the FREE information or tripwire offer will not remember who you are by dinner tonight.

So, during the time they register and the next step, I start sending them videos via email to help indoctrinate them, get them excited, and presell them.

Here is an example of my indoctrination campaign that I send people after they register. This example is for a webinar, but this same logic can be applied to any type of business. If you're a professional practice selling by appointment, remove the word webinar and insert consultation or appointment.

Each day leading to my webinar they get one video, and they can see the titles of the other videos coming up, so it gets them excited and keeps their attention.

Notice a few things.

In my case I push my "tripwire" offer again on each of these video pages.

I want to get them buying, because we know that a buyer in motion tends to stay in motion. I also like to have comments on the page for social proof, and I give them gifts to build reciprocity.

The one concern I always get from people when I show them the indoctrination sequence is this: "Russell, what if they register on Wednesday and they only get one or two of the indoctrination emails before the webinar?"

The answer is simple—the indoctrination sequence is not essential to the sale.

It's an amplifier. If they only see one video, and then they are on the webinar, that's okay.

Often videos two and three come after the webinar, and that's okay as well.

Often those videos will be the thing that pushes them over the edge in the follow-up sequences or gets them to actually watch the replays when they happen.

So don't stress about them not getting all of the videos before the webinar.

Most people won't, and that's okay because it's an amplifier, not an essential part of the sale.

Again, this doesn't just apply to webinars. Imagine if you're a local clothing boutique and you send all your paid traffic to your website, offering an instant coupon to shop at your store.

Then each season you create a seasonal fashion show. You set a date to stream a Zoom webinar or Facebook Live from your store, and you invite via email all of your customers and the people who have requested more information from your website to the live event.

For the week leading up to the event you send out a quick email with a link to a video from you highlighting just one piece or accessory that you'll display during the live show which could be thirty, sixty, ninety minutes, or more in length, where your single goal is to get your customers to buy!

Core Funnel #2: Webinar Funnel

I can hear it already, as you're reading this you're saying, "I own a restaurant, and my business is different. Russell this won't work for me."

Hold the phone.

During the early days of the COVID-19 pandemic, creative entrepreneurs around the world quickly figured out how to use webinars, Facebook Live, Zoom, and other platforms to get paid to deliver services virtually.

Webinar funnels are *not* just for online businesses. They are for all businesses, and the only limitation is the creativity of the business owner.

My fellow coauthor of this book, Darin Spindler, in addition to his highly successful Kids Bowl Free business also owns a restaurant. The restaurant was able to put together Pizza Kits and then do live classes including one with the Green Bay Packers families that were hosted on Zoom where they taught families how to make breadsticks, throw pizza dough, and enjoy an amazing pizza at home.

I shared how a clothing boutique can use webinar funnels, but we have smart business owners in dozens of industries including professional practices, personal trainers, health coaches, and many more quickly and easily integrate a webinar funnel into their businesses and maximize each and every lead that comes from the advertising dollars they invest.

Webinar funnels are usually selling something from $300 to $3,000.

Tripwire buyers get pushed into webinar funnels about seven to ten days after they have purchased the tripwire (about how long it takes them to get the tripwire shipped to them).

While a webinar funnel is usually focused on warmer traffic (i.e., people who have already bought your book or who are already on your list), we've found that if you use the perfect webinar script (that you can get for free at www.PerfectWebinarSecrets.com) many of our students have had great success promoting cold traffic directly into a webinar funnel because the ninety-minute webinar can actually move a prospect from cold to warm very quickly. I send cold traffic into my tripwire funnels and also my webinar funnels.

When they purchase a tripwire, I immediately start to ascend them up to the webinar funnels, and if they go through the webinar funnel first, then I focus on ascending them to my high-ticket funnels.

Core Funnel #3: High-Ticket Funnel

These are the funnels where I'm usually asking for anywhere from $3,000 to $100,000 or more.

It's very difficult to sell someone a $100,000 package online, so the high-ticket funnels move people from online to offline where you can sell the higher-end products and services on the phones.

If you want to go deep with high-ticket funnels, watch my webinar at www.HighTicketSecrets.com.

"Will this work in my business?"

Financial planner dude, you're selling your services on the phone and in person, right?

Use the high-ticket funnel to get prospects who are positioned and postured so when they get on the phone with you, they are begging to give you money instead of you trying to sell them.

"But I have all sorts of regulations. I can't sell financial products online..."

Then don't sell financial products online. In a high-ticket funnel, you're selling you; we never mention the product ... ever.

Okay ... rant over.

Oh wait, I forgot about the dentist and everyone else who said it won't work in their business because (fill in the blank with your excuse here) _____.

Dentist—a free teeth cleaning is a tripwire, and then use a webinar or live event funnel to move people toward high-ticket services like Invisalign, implants, or cosmetic dentistry.

Med Spas—a free Botox treatment is a tripwire, and then use a webinar or live event funnel to move people toward high-ticket services like CoolScuplting or cosmetic surgery options, for example.

There is no business that these three funnels won't work for.

As long as your company can benefit from leads and sales (and that should be everyone in business), then at least one of these three funnels will work for you (and typically all three will work even better).

As you can see, all other funnels eventually should be flowing to your high-ticket funnels. There are two reasons for this.

First, the most important reason, is that this is where you can give the biggest impact and results to your clients.

When people pay more, you have the ability to serve them at a higher level.

Also, at higher prices, people are typically more invested and more likely to have higher levels of success.

Second, this is where you make the most money. Typically higher-ticket products are almost all profit, especially when the lead acquisition costs have been covered in the lower funnels.

There are times that you can drive traffic directly to a high-ticket funnel, but usually the first time someone is introduced to our high-ticket funnel is with a very soft offer on the thank-you page of all of my tripwire and webinar funnels.

I don't sell it hard, but I want them to be aware of it and have it available for my hyperactive buyers who are ready for more.

The hook for the thank-you page ad is this: Would you like my help implementing what you just purchased?

That's the big secret. It's pretty simple, but it will get the right people to immediately raise their hands. It won't be a lot, usually only 1 to 2 percent of your buyers will move immediately to that option, but those people are often laydown sales.

Then over the next sixty days, our goal is to go from 1 to 2 percent of our buyers applying to 10 percent. At 10 percent applications, we have a formula that will give our high-end program the ability to scale quickly.

Use all of the information and tools that I share in my FREE sixty-seven-page report *The 3 Core Funnels & How They Work Together.*

Claim yours at www.FunnelStackingSecrets.com, where I go much deeper into this subject, and I also share a lot of the numbers to make the "money math" work for your business.

Using funnels in your business is a sure way to make sure that your Advertising Never Fails Again!

OVER THE PAST fifteen years, Russell has built a following of over a million entrepreneurs, sold hundreds of thousands of copies of his best-selling books, popularized the concept of sales funnels, and cofounded a software company called ClickFunnels that helps over one hundred thousand entrepreneurs quickly get their message out to the marketplace.

15

CHAPTER 15:

Ad Budgets Are Stupid

BUSINESS OWNERS AND executives are taught to set ad budgets. University professors teaching business teach ad budgets. Sometimes this budget setting is done as percentage of gross revenues, sometimes as a predetermined dollar amount (limit), sometimes for the year ahead, sometimes for each calendar quarter. They are set by some textbook formula or industry norm, or by using last year's facts and the coming year's desired growth. *In every case, they are stupid.* (Never forget: *most* industry norms, widely accepted practices taken for granted as sensible, and in-the-classroom exercises *are* stupid.)

$100 Bills, 50 Percent Off

Let us assume your bank is having a private sale for its customers, for seventy-two hours: $100 bills for $50. No rationing, no limits. Would you want to be restricted by a preset cap on the amount of money you can spend buying money at 50 percent off? How many times would you like to buy a stack of $100 bills for $50 each, then use them to buy more at 50 percent off, then use those to buy more? Answer: as many times as you could in the seventy-two hours, right? Ah, but if you are operating under a preset budget, you must stop. The stupidity of being forced to stop early by your own "budget" is obvious.

By the way, from time to time, ad media becomes available at such huge discounts that it is like buying $100 bills for $50. Very early on, TV infomercials made fortunes because TV stations shut down from midnight to 6:00 a.m., and that "dead time" could be bought for next to nothing. The buying advantage was short lived, of course, but while it lasted, it was as close to legal theft as you can get. During the worst months of the COVID-19 pandemic, TV advertising became a bargain, locally and nationally, as many usual heavy users of the media froze. Smart, aggressive business owners stepped in and snatched up that airtime. I know many who could not make TV advertising pay previrus who *did* make it pay off handsomely during the lockdowns.

Successful advertising *is* the buying of money at a discount. You buy a customer worth $100 for $50, as an example. If that's *not* what you're doing with your advertising, it's a damn good thing you found this book!

Barring capacity issues, you want to get advertising put together that works that way, then, *as fast as you can*, you want to spend on it, collect on it, spend what you collected, collect on that spend, spend the now-greater sum you collected, etc., etc. If the return on investment, in this example the $100 gained by every $50 spent, occurs over time but is certain, you may even want to borrow money to spend more, faster. Also, as I described, media bargains may present themselves, and if and when they do, you don't want some budget predetermined by a bean counter standing in your way of pouncing on it. **Preset budgets are for dopes. Return on investment and reinvestment for more of the same is the province of smart people.**

We can also compare advertising to human salespeople. (Advertising *is* "salesmanship by media.") If you put a sales rep out in the field, representing your company in Cleveland, and you conquer the math of that, making him productive and profitable, what should you do next? Replicate him in Columbus, Cincinnati, Pittsburgh, etc. as fast as you possibly can—not hemmed in by some preset budget for sales reps for the year ahead. In the Great Depression, as soon as W. Clement Stone figured out a methodical, successful approach for selling insurance by "cold" walk-in of offices in high-rise buildings, he recruited an army of salespeople as fast as he could to put the "system" to work in every office tower in Chicago, then New York, etc., taking advantage of the availability of "quality" people to sell door to door on commission created by the Depression. You can read his whole story in his book *The Success System That Never Fails*. He invested in human media, but the exact same reasoning applies to ad media.

This is *not* to suggest recklessness. This is about actual, factual measurement of ROI, return on investment.

> You have to *know* what you are getting for your ad dollar and when you are getting it.

You have to *know* what you are getting for your ad dollar and when you are getting it. That leans to direct-response advertising, not brand-building or image advertising. With direct response, you know day by day. With the other advertising, you *might* know quarter over quarter or year over year. The functional equivalent of source coded coupon redemption allows you to accurately count. The impact of brand awareness is almost impossible to count. You can't intelligently manage risk if you can't accurately count. But you can't think like a bean counter about it; you have to think like a bean grower. By the way, the reason people are bean counters is because they can't grow beans themselves! They are necessary in their roles, but they are *not* to be listened to about bean growing, nor is their math to be used for bean growing.

I know professional gamblers, mostly horse race bettors, who consistently succeed and have six-figure yearly incomes. I, myself, have a record of profit on days or nights at racetracks, betting seriously. What they and I know is that success is not just from picking winners. If you know how to read a racing form, that is actually not very hard. Success comes from careful management of whom you bet on, how you bet (win, place, show, exotics), how much you bet, factoring in odds, and when *not* to bet. Somewhat similarly, I would equate the message aspects of advertising to reading the racing form: you *can* learn how to do it, and it is *not* nuclear physics or brain surgery. But that alone won't produce success. One of the biggest "X factors" is with chosen media: when and how you buy … how much you pay.

16

CHAPTER 16:

Is *Successful* Advertising Art or Science?

BY NOW, YOU know the answer to that question.

There is a desire for it to be a "creative" process, to such an extent that in the advertising world, "creative" is used as a noun: the term for the ideas, copy and graphics, and "creatives" used as identity by the idea people, copywriters, and graphics technicians. The great ad man David Ogilvy criticized his peers for "worshipping at the altar of creative." When I entered advertising, I held this happy delusion, thinking of it as a wildly creative profession. *As "art."*

The realities of *successful* advertising are much different. Rather than the whole thing being wildly, joyously "creative," it is, instead, **"methodical."** It is more like dentistry or auto repair than it is art. There are, for example, well-established formulas and components to be cast aside in favor of new creativity at your peril.

The first person to assert the idea and truth of "scientific advertising" was Claude Hopkins, way, way back in 1923. His thin book titled *Scientific Advertising* was a manifesto, and at the time it enraged all the "creatives." It still does. If you force your web developer to read it, you risk causing his head exploding. Still, you *should* force him to read it. Out loud, to you.

In Hopkins's time, advertising was a very imperfect science, with data gathering difficult and results of testing slow. Hopkins would be perpetually orgasmic given today's tools, technology, and opportunities for fast assembly of results-based data.

Let's focus on the term "methodical" in place of "scientific"—it's not as intimidating, and it should be reassuring and motivational. You don't need "genius" to apply methodology; you need intelligence and discipline. This book has shown you that there *is* method to success with your advertising. It does *not* need to be a confusing jungle; there is a well-established path. It does *not* need to be a mysterious art, the province of mystics. *You can* understand it, and *you can* use and/or insist on a methodical approach.

I realize this *ruins the romance*. The romantic notion of several incredibly creative wizards locked in a room filled with marijuana smoke, emptied pizza boxes, whiteboards, and markers, spitballing ideas, ideas, ideas—until the brilliant slogan emerges that leads to world domination. Yes, I said earlier, it *is* best to have a Big Idea for your advertising message. But that is *one* element, not the entire game. And even it is more likely to come from a methodical approach to birthing a Big Idea than from random, spontaneous eruption.

Imposing Discipline on an Often-Undisciplined Process

One of the tools I've given you in this book is a small collection of *checklists*, with which to make advertising, and to judge advertising if developed for you by others. For your convenience, they are grouped together after the last chapter. It is useful to add to these as you find or learn other checklists.

I fly now only by private jet. I am always comforted by the pilot and copilot going through an organized checklist, out loud, before taxiing down the runway for takeoff. I'm sure they have talent; in a desperate emergency I'd love seeing it put on display, like Captain Sully safely landing the big airplane on the Hudson River. But other than in such an emergency, I'm *not* interested in having them improvise and be spontaneous or creative. I prefer the disciplined approach facilitated by checklists. With your advertising investments, you are flying your money. Better it not be an improvisational act.

When someone asks, "How was your flight?" I like to answer, "*Uneventful.*" That's the best kind of advertising and marketing system, performing each and every day in the same way, uneventfully, predictably. This can only be your reality if you insist on it and work toward *it* as your goal.

With this book I have done my level best to present advertising-marketing-sales-customer development in the context of system, not "silos" and in context of **organized** *effort*, not random, erratic acts. Most business owners, even most poor people, exert plenty of effort yet get disappointing results. Why? Because their effort is *not* well organized by objectives.

The other important thing I've attempted here is to have you understand the difference between *direct-response* advertising and

> **It's *your* money. I recommend *knowing* what you are doing with it, and I commend methodology over artistry.**

all other advertising; essentially, all others are often practiced as an art form, indulged at clients' expense, while direct response has its roots with Claude Hopkins, and is practiced as methodology. The great David Ogilvy once lashed out at the "creatives" in his agency, saying: "Only the direct-response people *know* what they are doing." It's *your* money. I recommend *knowing* what you are doing with it, and I commend methodology over artistry. **Never forget for a minute**: it *is your* money. *You* are responsible for it. It will be purposed or meandering, hard working or lazy, accountable or defying accountability by *your* controls.

I cannot urge strongly enough that you "hang out with," get information and guidance and leadership from and listen to "method advertisers" or "advertising scientists"—not romantics or mystics. This is a strong argument for your membership in No BS Inner Circle.

Jim Rohn said he could "psychically" predict your bank balance if given (1) a list of the books you've read and rank as important and the ones you are reading now, and (2) information about the five people you hang out with most and the five to twenty-five people you associate with and share ideas and information with most often. This is all about *the impact of association.*

The End. The Beginning.

This is the end of this book, and its revealing of why most advertising fails and how to make yours succeed. Hopefully, this will be the beginning of your taking the reins and remaking your business's advertising. Hopefully this will be the beginning of a new or more robust interest on your part in what makes successful, profitable advertising tick. It's as good a "money hobby" as any.

If you have found this book revelatory and productive, you will likely benefit by working your way through some or all of my other books, which you can find at Amazon and at NoBSBooks.com. You can also dip your toes further in the *system* water at MagneticMarketing.com.

If you wish to communicate with me directly, you are welcome to do so by fax: 330-908-0250 or mail or FedEx to 154 E. Aurora Road #353, Northfield, Ohio 44067. Note: I deliberately do *not* use email, social media, or text. Anything involving me you see online is from licensed, authorized publishers (or unauthorized pirates), not me, and communication directed to me to such sites never reaches me. Also, if you want a response from me, you need to furnish a fax number or physical address. I don't pick up the phone and call anybody; I don't email. I am essentially semiretired. I am active with marketing and business strategy consulting, but I no longer accept copywriting projects (with very rare exceptions). I travel reluctantly, and expensively, only by private jet, so most of the few speaking engagements I accept during a year tend to be placed in my primary home city, Cleveland, Ohio, or done by video or Zoom. However, I am happy to hear from readers of this or my other books.

So, What Do You *Now Know* about Succeeding with Advertising?

The biggest point is that advertising failures often aren't that at all; instead, they are failures to *integrate* the advertising into a complete *system* for attracting, developing, and retaining ideal customers and to properly purpose the advertising to start with. Often, probably 50 percent of the time, over all my years, new, would-be clients have come to me "to get a better ad." To me, this is like a child wanting pizza and ice cream for breakfast. I rarely permitted it. First, their entire business model had to be examined, the process a person responding to advertising went through, from first "raised hand" of interest to first transaction to postsale development, critically assessed and usually improved upon. This is on display in my book *Almost Alchemy: How to Get More from Fewer and Less.*

In part, this is about **financial efficiency**, important because *the* dirty little secret of advertising for business growth is that all fundamentals honored, the entity that can afford the highest cost (investment) to acquire a new customer, client, patient, or donor wins. **To be** *that* **advertiser; that one-thousand-pound King Kong competing with monkeys, you have to engineer high, comprehensive financial efficiency into your business, "from A to Z."** Otherwise, aggressiveness leads to bankruptcy. So, with almost every client, in order to give them the most powerful advertising strategy and ads, I had to guide them and coerce or compel them into reengineering the "internals" of their business. Advertising occurs externally. Its payoff, its return on investment, its winning or losing occurs internally. So, now you know what costs a lot of advertisers years and hundreds of thousands of dollars to figure out through what I call "expensive experience."

The second big thing you know is that with most types of businesses and most businesses, *it* is *the advertising*, and the entire marketing system, that makes the difference between below average, average, or exceptional growth, profit, and income, and equity value or created wealth. Not the products, not the services— in most categories and competitive environments, these are, bluntly, "me too." Most furniture stores mostly sell the same furniture; it is their advertising, and their entire advertising-marketing-selling system that separates them financially, into a pyramid, with one at the very top, a few right beneath them, a fat middle group barely doing okay, and a wide bottom where struggle just to survive plays out. Same with personal injury law firms, chiropractic practices, and just about any other business in each local or area market. The Money Pyramid is there, and it is the advertising and the full system fed by it that determines who is where on that pyramid. Therefore, *you did exactly the right thing* by getting and reading this book, by being interested in mastering advertising. If you believe in "follow the money," *this* is where the money is.

Now, the pregnant question is: What *actions* will you take next, in response to the knowledge and understanding gained? *All* success is created by first information, creating awareness, then decision, then action. Most stop short. They quickly settle back into familiar, habitual practices, rather than grabbing any bull by its horns. Here, I'm out of the equation. Hopefully, I've provided provocative information and have made you newly or clearly or acutely aware of opportunities to substantially strengthen the advertising and marketing of your business. I can't take action for you, nor can I assume responsibility for it. What's next is all on you. Your customers and their value are your fault. Your system or lack thereof is yours to live with as is or dig into and improve or, if need be, replace. Whether you go ahead and connect with No BS Inner Circle and its Magnetic Marketing System® and related support or not is 100 percent your decision. You *have* stepped forward and are to be congratulated for it. Most business owners do *not* have "improvement curiosity." They often mutter to themselves, "There *must* be a better way," but they do not use that as impetus to investigation, to search for the better way! You have. Good! Now, what *will* you do next?

CHAPTER 17:

The Top Ten Songs That Will Tell You Why Advertising Fails and How to Make Yours Succeed

by Marty Fort

I'M A MUSICIAN and music teacher with over thirty years of performance and teaching experience. I'm also a longtime student of Dan Kennedy, having worked with him as a private client for more than a decade. He has been invaluable in helping me develop my brick-and-mortar businesses, as well as my coaching and licensing businesses. He has greatly shaped the way I think about and understand advertising. So, I'm so glad you're reading this book and taking this opportunity to fix your advertising, because he will fix it!

I'm going to break down his marketing for you from a musician's perspective to make it fun. Because a huge part of marketing is just that: making it fun! Here's a top-ten list of songs that'll explain to you in detail of why your advertising is failing and how to make it succeed "Dan's Way."

Song Number One: You're So Vain, You Probably Think This Ad Is about You ("You're So Vain" by Carly Simon)

Most business owners, when they look at their marketing, don't look at it for what it's truly designed to do. What marketing is designed to do is to produce a result. It is designed purely to procure a customer. To send out a marketing dollar and get a sales dollar back. It is a mechanism, not a piece of art. If you take the composer Mozart, for example: he was not just writing music with his heart on his sleeve for free. He would only write music if he had a commission, which means the money had to be up front and ready to go in advance. Then he would compose a piece. You had to show Mozart the money!

But what happens with an ad is a business owner views it as a vanity piece versus as a way to acquire a customer. They'll make a website, they'll make a print ad and then focus solely on the aesthetics. They focus on the color scheme. They focus on things that frankly don't matter like artsy aesthetics, branding, etc. That's not Kennedy-style direct-response marketing. Branding is not what's going to produce results for the small business owner.

> **Your ads can still be pleasant to the eye and sophisticated, but they have to primarily serve as a way to get a customer to directly respond.**

What produces results is, without a doubt, Dan Kennedy–style direct-response marketing.

It works for financial advisors. It works for attorneys. It works for churches. It works online and in print.

Your ads can still be pleasant to the eye and sophisticated, but they have to primarily serve as a way to get a customer to directly respond. If your advertising is pretty to look at, but it's not communicating with people, that's why it's failing. If your ads are not direct response with an offer, headline, grabbing attention—all of the things that Dan Kennedy teaches us—those are further reasons why your advertising's failing. But the good news is this book will give you the solutions to fix your advertising (and quick).

If you're honest with yourself, you know the human condition is steered and controlled by our ego not our logic. We come from a natural position that our marketing should be some form of art. There is an art to direct-response selling, but the ads themselves are not pieces of art per se. Unless you're Bob Ross, that's not how the money is made.

So, if you're going to be a business owner and make your ads succeed, you've got to get your vanity out the door and realize this ad is not about you. What this ad is about is providing a solution to the customer, making them aware of a problem, and giving them a limited time to respond and multiple ways to respond. Then a sale is made. That's how your fix your advertising

Song Number Two: "Throwing it All Away" (Genesis)

I've seen this happen over and over again. You'll go to a Kennedy event, read one of Dan's books, maybe watch a video of him speaking, etc. You'll great ideas, make a great direct-response ad with the items listed in song number one. You're good to go. But then a very bad thing occurs. It's what Dan calls NIOP, which is the "Negative Influence of Other People." This is a real phenomenon. And I've seen it thousands of times because I've been a business coach myself for over a decade. I'll fix somebody's website, or I'll fix their print ad, or I'll fix whatever marketing they've been screwing up. Then they go home and their wife or their husband who thinks they are a marketing genius (or worse, an ad agency gets ahold of them), and the client changes everything back and throws it all away. They undo the fixed ad and make something pretty to satiate their friends, their family, and their ego. But they won't make a dime from their revised ad. They have literally not only thrown the ad away but also their opportunity for a sale.

You've got to tune out the noise. Lebron James, the NBA basketball player, said that to Zion Williams in his rookie year, meaning he needs to tune out those saying things to distract him and get in the way of his success. After you've made your new Kennedy-style ads, if you have people advising you that are saying, "That's an ugly ad ... you should do this instead," or "You can't say that!" ask yourself these questions:

How many customers do they have?

Do they have a merchant account?

Do they have a business license?

Have they ever made a sale in their life?

Well, if you're listening to your uncle, who is a professor or your spouse who's never owned a business in their life, I'm sure they're wonderful people. But they're in no way qualified to advise you on marketing. And if you go through an ad agency, as Dan will tell you, the way ad agencies make money is by selling ads on your behalf. They get a commission. By nature it's an adversarial relationship. They don't have your best interest at heart. Who you listen to matters (a lot). So don't make a great ad and then throw it all away. It's a real thing, I'm telling you.

Song Number Three: Your Marketing Isn't Talking Loud and It Ain't Saying Nothing ("Talkin' Loud and Sayin' Nothing" by James Brown)

That kind of goes back to song number one. I mean, the big thing is that most people are wired because of vanity to want to make their advertising pretty. They view it as a representation of their personality, their image, their persona, and so on. But again, that's not the purpose of marketing. It's one of the main reasons why your advertising is failing. To make it succeed, your advertising has to serve as a communication conduit. It's needs to speak directly, swiftly to what's going on in the customer's mind. It needs to provide solutions and then build a sense of urgency to act. If you're looking at your advertising and it's very brandish, it's not really communicating to your clients. Ask yourself what's going through their mind. What is keeping them up at night? All of the stuff Dan Kennedy teaches us.

Let me be a broken record (no pun intended). A primary reason your marketing is not bringing you the results you desire is it's talking loud, but it ain't saying nothing. Marketing is about a conversation with a sale at the end. Not a piece of art to frame and hang on the wall.

Song Number Four: Unchain My Stats ("Unchain My Heart" by Joe Cocker)

This is a play on "Unchain My Heart." Most business owners don't have a clue what their stats are in terms of how much they're spending and how much they're getting back from their marketing. Additionally, most ad agencies will try to skew the results to make them look better at what they do. Google does this. Facebook also does this. The online media rep will show you impressions to beef up their "success stats." But as you know, impressions don't translate into cash sales. Actual cash sales is what we track and is the most important metric. I'll tell you some stories from different radio experiences I've had as an advertiser.

I went to a radio station to tape a commercial. Being a Kennedy-style direct-response guy, at the end of the commercial, I added a tracking tag to the script. A simple "mention this station and get X off by such a date." In horror the engineer and radio ad reps shut the whole recording down.

Literally, three radio executives rushed in and said, "You can't do that! It's against company policy."

They were earnest in their attempt to pressure me into taking that part out of the script, which I told them in no uncertain terms, I was not going to do.

I said, "I can just leave right now."

So, because I stood my ground, they caved and left the tag in. But the reason they do that is *they don't want you to track their numbers.* They don't want you to see how miserable the response to their media can be.

So, one of the reasons your advertising is failing is you're not keeping track of the stats. The sellers of the media are certainly not keeping track. Everybody's just hoping that you're going to be fat, oblivious, dumb, and happy. In my situation word got out to the other stations about how I think as a marketer. I went to a different radio station and taped a commercial with the same script. When I got home later that day, they sent me the final edit and said, yeah, "We had to take that tag out. Sorry." So, they changed the terms after the fact, assuming that I would give up having gone through the trouble of taping the spot.

I said, "Ok, cancel the ads."

You've got to stand your ground, and you will face adversity from many: The same adversity you have from people trying to negatively influence you to change your ads and make them pretty again. The same brand advertising proponents that do not speak loudly in their ads. Look, this is extremely important. Sales is how we feed our families. This is how we get to have nice homes and accumulate money so we can give it to whomever we want to in life. You can keep it, you can give money to your church, a charity, whatever you want to do with it, but it's your choice. Through my businesses I've given over $100,000 to the pet rescue, Pets Inc. They named their onsite emergency room "The Marty Fort Critical Care Unit."

My point?

I couldn't have achieved that without Dan's kind of marketing.

But the problem is as marketers our egos get in the way.

1. We listen to others and let them influence us,

2. We're not really communicating to the customer. We're just kind of throwing our name out there.

3. We're not tracking our stats.

4. So let's "Unchain Our Stats" and our wallets at the same time.

Song Number Five:
One Is the Loneliest Number
("One" by Three Dog Night)

This is one of the biggest takeaways I've learned from Dan. The worst number in business is one. I've actually seen people wear this as a badge of honor, and I hate it. They'll say to me in a boastful fashion, "I don't advertise." Their attitude is they don't have to advertise. They don't have to go on the hunt for a customer, which in the end is suicide, and it's going to catch up to them eventually. It's like somebody who smokes three packs a day and thinks that's not going to matter—until one day the medical report comes in, and it does matter. Or the bank account is empty, and of course it matters.

So, you've got the crowd that doesn't advertise at all and is proud of it, which is why their advertising's failing: because there is none. Or just about as bad, they're only doing one thing to market to customers. They're a doing website, and that's about it. Or they rely on word of mouth and nothing else. But what Dan teaches us is diversity leads to stability. The way I've been able to grow my brick-and-mortar businesses and grow my coaching businesses is by having a diverse portfolio of online and print marketing. So, if you want to make your advertising work, instead of doing just one thing, create a marketing plan with twenty, thirty, forty things that you're doing every month to acquire and retain customers. That's what leads to stability.

Song Number Six: Just Another Manic Monday—and for You, *Every Day* Is a Manic Monday ("Manic Monday" by The Bangles)

This is so true of people I've worked with as clients, people in my family, and people that are my friends. Their advertising is failing because they are living their life under the excuse of "The Busy Card." They've got family problems, health problems, employee problems, client problems, tax problems, time management problems, divorce problems, mental problems, problems, problems, problems. Did I mention they have problems?

And they're just too busy because of this to devote any time, effort, or resources to marketing. Their daily fires take up all of their attention.

Currently I own and operate three brick-and-mortar music lesson schools, grossing over $2 million per year in sales. I also own the buildings for each. My coaching business works with hundreds of coaching clients on six continents that I coach monthly. I host live seminars in major cities and a licensing program that serves forty thousand music students and has nine patents. As a business owner, I have fifteen full-time employees and eighty contractors that report to me, not to mention a wife that I love, a six-year-old daughter that I'm dedicated to, and four dogs—and I still play in a band. Recently I got to perform on stage with Kirk Hammett from Metallica, one of the biggest bands in the world. So, I not only play in a band; I play in a band at a very high level.

The bottom line is I burned my Busy Card a long time ago. *My Mondays are manic too*. So how can you do the same? My favorite Dan Kennedy No BS® book, is the *Ruthless Management of People and*

Profits. If you're going to make your advertising work, you've got to get your systems down so your time is freed up to focus on creating great ads. Like me, you've got to burn your Busy Card. You've got to shift your focus, which leads us to song number seven.

Song Number Seven: "The Show Must Go On" (Queen)

> To make your advertising work, you've got to realize we've all got problems, but the show must go on, and *the show is marketing.*

In one way or another, the show *is* marketing. At a recent Music Academy Success® conference in Nashville for our music school clients, I told the attendees, "You are not in the music school business." Dan will tell you, and he's right, you are in the marketing business. But I would add, and I told the audience, you're also in the *"perennial problem business."* Jerry Richardson, the founder of the Carolina Panthers, said, "If you don't have problems, you don't have a business."

To make your advertising work, you've got to realize we've all got problems, but the show must go on, and *the show is marketing*. Advertising is everything.

Advertising is what brings in cash flow, clients, and, ultimately, freedom—which leads us to song number eight.

Song Number Eight: "Freedom" (Richie Havens)

If you're going to have true business and financial freedom and make your advertising work, you've got focus on marketing and cash flow. Cash in a lot of ways solves all (or at least a lot). The person who said, "Money doesn't buy happiness" *didn't have any money*. There's a dangerous rise in what the author and thought leader Ayn Rand called the "Veil of Altruism," meaning that people want to be seen as selfless. They want to put on this front that everything they do is for everyone else and not themselves.

Don't ever be ashamed of wanting to make money and enjoying the freedom it brings. But that freedom only comes from fixing your advertising. Broken advertising equals a broke business owner.

The bottom line of business is really simple. Cash is king. If the cash flow is there, you can pretty much figure everything else out. You can fix systems. You can fix software that comes and goes. You can get new employees. You can get whatever it is that you need. True freedom is fixing your advertising Kennedy style and improving your cash flow.

Song Number Nine: "Rock You Like a Hurricane" (Scorpions)

If you study Dan from his work during the '70s until now, you'll quickly get that is he is a force of nature. He is not timid. I've been fortunate enough to do multiple live events with him in Cleveland for my music school owners. We did one at Disney via Zoom for our top Music Academy Success® members. He said to me, *"Marty, you know, the trick with your guys is they're timid."* And he's right. I think a lot of business owners fall under that category. So, what's his point?

The point is the reason your advertising is failing is because it **isn't rocking anyone like a hurricane**. It's timid, pretty, middle of the road—it's vanilla. No headline, no offer, no deadline to respond, no rock and roll!

If you're going to make it succeed, you've got to ask yourself …

Are you rocking your clients and your advertising like a hurricane?

Are you going right to their pain points?

Going to right what's going through their head?

Solving their needs?

Screaming to get their attention like somebody on the floor of the Wall Street Stock Exchange.

That's what you've got to do. You've got to turn up the volume!

Song Number Ten: "Seek and Destroy" (Metallica)

One of the things I love about Dan is he's an aggressive guy. He's an aggressive coach, marketer, entrepreneur, and teacher, and he shows us that we are here to seek and destroy with our advertising. With every ad campaign we do, we are here to aggressively seek out more clients, destroy the competition, and have a passion for direct-response marketing.

It's not about just having a logo. It's not about having a vanity piece. It's not about getting distracted by others. It's not about just having branding. It's not about being distracted by ad reps. It's not about tracking. And it's certainly not about doing just one thing (or worse, nothing). It's about going out to seek and destroy with the techniques of direct-response marketing, Dan Kennedy style.

Bonus Track:
"Eruption" (Van Halen)

The bonus track I have for you is "Eruption," which was Van Halen's first song on their first album.

When Eddie Van Halen came out with the guitar tapping technique used on this song, it revolutionized the guitar-playing world.

If you leave this chapter and become really dedicated to laying down everything I've gone through with you, everything Dan's going through with you, and all the other coauthors, then you can have your own marketing eruption. ***Your own personal marketing revolution.***

So, get out there, be prepared to seek and destroy, rock your advertising like a hurricane, have the freedom to improve your cash flow and run your business. Always know the show must go on, and look … every day is a manic Monday.

Get over it.

Burn your Busy Card.

Stop having just one marketing thing.

Unchain your stats.

Get your marketing talking loud.

Make it say something!

Stop throwing it all away once you've fixed it.

Stop making something and then letting somebody talk you out of it.

And please don't be so vain. This ad is not about you.

It's about ***kicking ass and taking names Dan Kennedy style.***

MARTY FORT
CEO Music Academy Success®
Author of *The Ultimate Guide to Music Lessons*
www.MusicAcademySuccess.com

patients or customers and keep them coming back to your office while keeping the back door locked so they will not leave, the faster your business will grow.

Here is a short story that illustrates this principle:

It was an early, cloudy morning in Southern California when I drove into the office parking lot and saw that there was a line of patients waiting outside the door.

Today was our Annual Free Dentistry Day, when we usually treat veterans and families of disadvantaged backgrounds. I have been offering this for several years as a way to give back to the communities I've served for almost three decades.

My first patient told me that he drove one hour to the office and had been waiting for us to open since 5:00 a.m. We discussed his medical history and took an X-ray of his mouth. He had a bombed-out upper molar, which I drilled and took out in pieces. While I apologized to him for the amount of time it took to do this, I did not tell him that I usually have my in-house oral surgeon do these procedures, and I was a bit "rusty."

The patient was grateful, said, "Thank you," and left. I distinctly remember this patient because six months later, he came back for more treatment and invested more than $10,000 in his oral health, including several implants.

I share this story because I know the patient did not come back for my clinical skill. He came back because our team showed that we cared, and I treated him with dignity on our Free Dentistry Day.

If a patient comes in for free the first time and stays to make a large financial investment, our job is to assess how to make *that* kind of a return visit a focus of our business growth.

I am proud that I have built a business that has families coming to my clinic who are in their third generation of care with me: grandparents, parents, and young children. I also have many patients who have been coming to me regularly for more than twenty-four years. I am honored to share three Magnetic Marketing strategies that I use to create that kind of longevity and loyalty in my practice.

1. Know Your Metrics

First, we need to know the basic metrics, the acquisition cost of a new patient, the average value of a new patient, the lifetime value of a patient, and how long each patient has been with us and then *educate* our team so each person in the office understands the maximum value of a patient.

For example, if we spent $50 to acquire a customer through Facebook ads, and the new patient spends an average of $1,500, we should be frustrated to find out our staff answered (or did not answer!) the phone and failed to book the appointment. We just lost $50 in marketing and potential income of at least $1,500. If an average patient stays with us for five years and spends $1,500 per year, then when a patient does not make that initial booking, the loss of potential income is more than $7,500 for that patient *plus* the value of any family member and friends that patient may refer.

When we do this math and share with our staff, it is very easy to show them *why* it is important to keep an existing client. This helps you encourage the staff to put up with Mr. Jones's temper, since he's been a patient for ten years and refers everyone he knows. They will also be flexible and allow Mrs. Smith to bring her kid in ten minutes late to his orthodontic appointment, because she has five kids who will need braces, and she is a large potential referral source, since she chairs the middle school PTA.

On a side note, before I make a decision such as "Can we give Dorothy a discount because she just broke a tooth and needed a $5,000 implant?" I always look her up in the ledger, check her lifetime value-to-date, and use that information to make the decision.

People may say, "That's very money oriented and not 'good patient care.'" In reality, I know my business metrics, make decisions based on numbers, and grow my business based on the 80/20 rule, where I know 20 percent of my patients bring in 80 percent of my income. Therefore, I give "preferential treatment" to the 20 percent. After all, how can I give "good patient care" to anyone if my business is not successful?

2. Be Present and Be Known

Secondly, you need to position yourself as an expert, the go-to person to provide your particular service in your community. Patients coming to you already expect you to be competent. You need to invest in additional training, whether in clinical or business, and *communicate* your expertise to your patients. Otherwise, you will be the "best-kept secret."

Take the time to think about your passion and expertise, and then make plans to share it. There are several ways to share. You can write articles and submit them to professional publications or a community newspaper. You can teach webinars or do lunch-and-learns to promote new services. The possibilities are endless.

Hosting and sponsoring events is one of my favorites. We invite our patients to an Annual Movie Night, where I rent out an entire movie theater, and patients can enjoy popcorn and drinks and watch a blockbuster with family and friends. We encourage the patients to invite guests, some of whom may be prospects and will consequently become patients.

Right before the movie starts as a private screening, our team shares new services and procedures provided in the office and asks for testimonials from preselected patients. The entire event is planned out in detail because we know we have a captive audience who like us, and we know the potential value in the audience. We always get a positive return on our investment from prospects becoming new patients and existing patients coming in for more treatment after this event.

Every year, I also host Patient Appreciation Dinner, where we invite our VIP patients for the past twelve months. The VIP criteria is determined by how much they have invested in their oral health during that period of time, usually at least $5,000. I am always humbled to walk into a room of ten to fifteen families and know that they had spent several hundred thousand dollars with us in the past 12 months.

When I share these tried-and-proven strategies at different seminars, the most frequent questions are, "Isn't that too much money for you to spend?" and "How can you be sure you do not lose money?" My answers to these questions are always about tracking and planning. We email the tickets, tracking the people who registered for the movie, so we know exactly who comes to the event, and who the new business comes from as a result. During the preshow, we share great information about our services and have live testimonials right in the theater. We know we will have prospects turning into new clients, and inactive patients returning to the office simply because of the Rule of Reciprocity.

As you do these powerful things in your business, whether staying at the cutting edge of technology, getting additional training in clinical expertise, or hosting wonderful events, you want to share it with the community and be featured in the media as much as possible. You want to stand out and not be just "the doctor down the street." We always announce and share our activities in the community through local newspapers, press releases, podcasts, etc., so we are always "present" and remembered. In other words, we show up, and I recommend that you show up, too.

As healthcare providers, we also need to constantly communicate with our patients about their health and how much we care for them and inform them about updates to our office. This goes beyond the automated texts and emails campaigns. We use the *mLive* software program to send continuous, targeted educational material explaining the importance and benefits of needed treatments and inviting the patients to make appointments. We share stories in our newsletter, a form of media content we can create and control. With newsletters, we can offer promotions and share cool gossip, such as how ten of our patients are graduating from high school this summer, or how Mr. Smith just retired after thirty-five years working at the post office.

> We create a community–as Dan Kennedy calls it, "the herd"–and we become a part of our patients' lives. People buy from people they know, like, trust, and agree with.

In short, we create a community—as Dan Kennedy calls it, *"the herd"*—and we become a part of our patients' lives. People buy from people they know, like, trust, and agree with.

By being present, we constantly remind our patients that we are there for them, encouraging them to keep up their recall appointments. By constantly introducing new and updated information and treatment options, we encourage patients to come in for more treatments, thus increasing the frequency of visits and the size of purchase. This combination of patient-care strategies helps us maximize the patient lifetime value and is the best way to grow our professional practice.

3. Be a Great Personality

The third way to connect with patients and increase their trust is to show your unique personality, because *you do your best.*

In my office, I have my books framed and hung on the wall, right under my professional certificates. There are also two framed articles and magazine cover stories about my life coming to the US as a refugee from Vietnam and various other acknowledgements of community achievements over the years. This helps the patient connect to me as a person, not just a professional.

There is a green jar on the front counter with a tight lid that is labeled "Ashes of Problem Patients." We also have a sign on the bathroom door: "All Men Are Created Equal. That Is Why Women Are in Charge." So, as the patients walk back to the operatories, already giggling from reading the signs, they expect a relaxed appointment and a fun-loving, slightly sarcastic dentist. When I provide great service and overdeliver on their expectations, even in the sarcasm department, I win patients for life!

I challenge you to go and check out what's on your wall or on the counter in your office, and ask yourself, "Why are those items there?" Are they just random items or intentionally conveying a message? My training with Magnetic Marketing taught me to be very intentional and to conduct business in such a way as to keep the patient and win a relationship. The sale, or production, is a byproduct of this particular system.

Many years ago, we had a fun patient, Ms. Angela, who would always come to the office beautifully dressed: wavy red hair, great makeup, colorful scarf, and fancy jewelry. She was in her seventies. She would show up for her checkups and prophylaxis religiously, so she never needed much in the way of major treatments. Remember the lifetime value of a patient we discussed previously? Well, it wasn't much with Ms. Angela.

One day, out of curiosity, I asked, "Where do you go after the dental appointment? You always dress so nicely!"

"Oh, I dress up to see y'all!" she replied with a big smile. We were happy and impressed with the love she showed us every time she came in.

At one of her visits, I took a picture of her with my then newly bought point-and-shoot camera and printed the photo right in the office to give to her. She was posing next to a big smile poster and was ecstatic to get the photo!

Several months later, her son called the office to let me know she had passed away. "The reason for my call, Dr. Letran," he said, "is as the family went through her things, we found a black notebook titled *Angela's Favorite Things*. Your name, Dr. Emily, was on that list of favorite things."

I choked up with emotion. We all know we touch our patients' lives over the years. Sometimes, with all the bustle and chaos in the office, we forget that it is a privilege to be part of their lives.

Are you part of your customers' list of favorite things?

4. The Next Step

You can run a lean and mean office and be the most effective business in marketing. You can implement several *Magnetic Marketing* strategies, targeting the right demographics who are most likely to become your patients. You can use marketing systems like *mLive* to nurture relationships in an effective, automated way without losing the personal touch. Once the patient comes into the office, how you impress that patient and keep in touch with them will keep that patient with you for life.

When patients become part of your office, know you, and trust you, they will be more open to buy whatever services you offer. From a basic bread-and-butter practice, you can offer clear aligners therapy, sleep apnea, cosmetic dentistry, implant dentistry … all higher-dollar-value services, immediately increasing your profit margin and the size of purchase. You can bring in specialists who provide services you don't like to do or don't want to learn to do. In the same eight-hour day, with multiple chairs and multiple providers, you will increase your collection number by offering higher-dollar services and bundles of service packages, thus increasing your dollar value per sale.

Last, but not least, you can grow your business by increasing the frequency of purchase. Some people make a sale and forget about what is available after. I advise you to build a strong relationship and find out as much about your patients and customers as possible so that you can offer more services catered just to them.

Marketing and growing a business should be a well-designed system with tweaks and adaptations along the way, much like your other precise professional procedures that took you years to refine. Treating your business like a business and taking care of your customers like family will help you accelerate your business growth,

19

CHAPTER 19:

An Extra Afterthought, Raised by the Pandemic

I WROTE MOST of this book in the tenth, eleventh and twelfth month of the China Virus's invasion and its terrible damage to our nation, including businesses' destruction. Along with just about everybody else, I was surprised by China's naked irresponsibility (if not more nefarious behavior), surprised by the epic spread, and surprised by the quick power-grabbing and tyrannical and arbitrary wielding of it by governors and mayors. There has been a lot to be surprised about. There may be more yet to come.

What did *not* **surprise me was**, with a few category exceptions, those wounded the worst and the fastest were the businesses most dependent on "1-step" advertising to produce day-to-day revenues; those businesses engaged in transactions, not in relationships. Those living off "traffic"—not well-maintained contact lists and multimedia use of them—got to Empty fast. Conversely, those driven by

COMPLETE Marketing Systems were best able to convert some or all of their lead management, selling, and customer retention to online and digital places, like Zoom, and to full-blown e-commerce. Even in the very tough category of restaurants prohibited from indoor dining, those with email, mail, and phone lists and previously maintained relationships were able to convert to and "pump up" take-out, ready-to-heat, delivery, mini food stores, even online cooking classes and other activities. For many, this provided only emergency survival, not prosperity, but that has been a lot better than financial death. Also, many businesses with complete marketing systems were able to capitalize on ad media bargains, locally and nationally, and *increase* sales and market share. For them, advertising could be made to pay, while, for direct competitors, it could not be used at all. Paraphrasing Rockefeller, they bought advertising when there was blood in the streets.

I am pleased to say that entire "tribes" of different kinds of businesses whose coaches and advisors are my clients—including law firms, dental practices, financial advisors, music schools, and others—as well as MOST of the Members of NO BS INNER CIRCLE in a wide diversity of businesses have done well so far in these difficult and confusing times. Many rebounded from the shocking punch in the nose quickly, and have reported reductions in revenue, profit, and retained teams of as little as 10 to 20 percent. Many are even up, year over year. This is, in part, because they already had in place a COMPLETE SYSTEM that allowed them to adapt, and in part because of

> **Serious challenges and disruptions actually occur *with regularity*. You actually have no right to be taken by surprise!**

their already-cultivated mindset about being a successful entrepreneur. They were *ready to be resilient.*

This point is extremely important: being ready to be resilient. You could not have predicted the China Virus let loose, the shutdown of the economy, etc. This *specific* challenge and disruption to your business's success and stability was unforeseeable. But, **broadly, serious challenges and disruptions actually occur** *with regularity.* You actually have no right to be taken by surprise!

At least every decade, we have a major national one: a 9/11, violent civil unrest in major cities, a steep and deep recession. Locally and regionally, challenges and disruptions occur much more frequently, from the main road to your business being ripped up and under reconstruction for a year; to tornadoes and hurricanes, fires and floods; to a major area employer closing its doors and putting half the town out of work. In different industries and professions, new government regulation and interference can descend. Online, the chief media—Google, Facebook, Twitter—can suddenly and arbitrarily impose new rules, can ban an entire type of advertising, can suppress search in a category. But that is not unique to online; I have had full-page ads running profitably in national magazines suddenly banned. Entire media can be taken away—for example, "cold" tele-prospecting, by Do-Not-Call-List laws, by broadcast fax outlawed.

> The harsh reality is that it is your fault, if you are not prepared to be resilient, and for your business to be resilient.

I am sixty-six years old, and with exception of one year as an employee, I have been an entrepreneur every year after short pants. I have seen, experienced, been confronted by, and/or worked intimately with clients or entire groups of businesses confronted by every one of the adversities I've just listed. And others. Multiple times. If you hope to "cruise" to success, it better be a damn short cruise.

The harsh reality is it *is* your fault, if you are not prepared to be resilient, and for your business to be resilient. Really smart work, on your business, on your advertising, marketing, selling—as a system, not separate islands or, worse, random acts—and, frankly, on your mindset features building and preparing to withstand foreseeable and specifically unforeseeable challenges and disruptions. This is practical application of "only the strongest survive." This book has been about more than advertising per se. It has been about *becoming "strong."* If you are not, the first vital thing to do is admit it. Identify your fragilities and vulnerabilities, prioritize them, and get to work replacing them with strengths. Today. There is always SOME thing you can do, now, and you want to do the doable. The second thing to do (probably) is to get experience-based, relevant help, guidance, support, and tools, to speed your progress. Whatever you do, do NOT ignore, deny, or accept weakness.

DAN S. KENNEDY

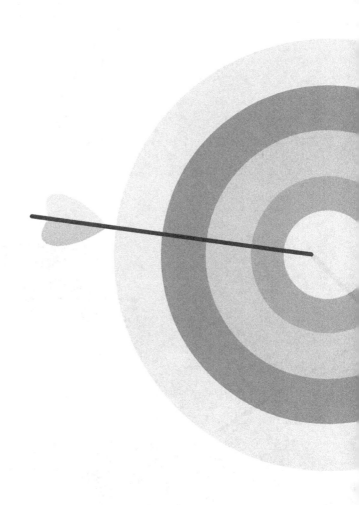

CHECK LISTS

FOUR TYPES OF ADVERTISING IN THE ADVERTISING TOOLBOX

(*Not* in any order of preference or comparative virtue)

1. Brand Awareness/Image
2. One-Step Sale (Only) for the "Buy *Now*" Customer
3. Lead Generation/Multistep
4. Hybrid

* * *

THE FOUR ADVERTISING *ESSENTIALS*

1. News
2. Promise of Benefit (One or the other or both nearly always presented for the first time in the ad's headline.)
3. Claim of Comparative or Competitive Superiority
4. Call to Specific Action Immediately

* * *

ADVERTISING NEEDS TO TELL PEOPLE

1. exactly what you want them to do next;
2. what will occur when they do;
3. why it is of benefit to them to do it;
4. why it is timely or urgent to do it immediately.

* * *

DO YOU *KNOW* AND CAN YOU RECITE THESE THREE CONVERSATIONS OF YOUR CUSTOMERS?

1. At the kitchen table at dinner

2. At the kitchen table, in the middle of the night when one spouse who couldn't sleep has come downstairs and the other notices, follows, and insists on knowing what's bothering him or her

3. In the car, on the way home from an afternoon or evening at their adult children's house

* * *

THE THREE HURDLES

1. Disinterest
2. Skepticism
3. Resistance

* * *

HOW TO COUNTER DISINTEREST

(1) Specific, (2) obvious, and, ideally, (3) timely or urgent relevance is the best cure for disinterest.

* * *

WHAT PEOPLE ARE (REALLY) INTERESTED IN

F amily

O ccupation

R ecreation

M oney

Never Again Be An Advertising Victim, Discover The Secrets To Creating A <u>Successful Advertising and Marketing System</u> For Your Business, Products and Services...

Get *THE* System That Business Owners Just Like You Have Used To Radically Transform Their Advertising From Ineffective and Wasteful Into A Business Asset That Will <u>Predictably and Reliably Deliver A Steady Stream Of New Customers, Clients, Patients and</u> *<u>Profits to the Bottom Line!</u>*

In This Master Class, You'll Discover:

❩ The difference between **Lead Generation** and **Brand Building**, and why lead generation almost always **TRUMPS** the latter.

❩ In most cases, THIS one form of advertising is only **wasting your time and money** for <u>**minimal results.**</u>

❩ THIS form of advertising will have you <u>**seeing returns in days, weeks, or months**</u> instead of wondering what the expense brought to you in return a year down the road.

❩ How YOU can be successful <u>**without having to worry about how many people know your brand by name.**</u>

❩ Learn how advertising in certain media outlets that have <u>**nothing**</u> to do with your business can actually make **A LOT** of sense and be <u>**very beneficial.**</u>

❩ How to <u>**model**</u> the marketing strategies of national companies in a way that will **translate their success into a <u>local level.</u>**

4 Amazing Bonus Gifts Valued at $938.97

Bonus Gift 1:
FREE Lead Generation Advertising Mastery Video Master Class
$297.00 Value

Bonus Gift 2:
The Best Of Dan Kennedy Collection
$497.97 Value

Bonus Gift 3:
Dan Kennedy's 10 Rules Of Direct Response Advertising Check List
$47.00 Value

Bonus Gift 4:
30 Day *FREE Trial* of the 'Famous' No B.S. Marketing Newsletter and Magnetic Marketing Gold Membership
$97.00 Value

Request Instant FREE Access At www.WhyAdvertisingFails.com/Gift

About the Author

DAN S. KENNEDY sat on the corner of his dad's drawing board as a wee lad, watching advertising being assembled. He has, in one way or another, been involved with advertising his entire life. He has been a serial entrepreneur, a strategic advisor and consultant, and one of America's highest-paid freelance advertising copywriters. He also enjoyed twenty years at the top of the speaking profession, repeatedly sharing the platform with other top business speakers like Zig Ziglar, Jim Rohn, Brian Tracy, and Tom Hopkins as well as celebrity entrepreneurs like Debbi Fields (Mrs. Fields Cookies), Jim McCann (1-800-Flowers), and Donald Trump. Dan is the author of more than thirty business books as well as coauthor of two mystery novels, all available at Amazon and other booksellers. Today, he consults and teleconsults with a small cadre of entrepreneur clients and is a content contributor to Magnetic Marketing's media.

Grow your business with

MAGNETIC
MARKETING

Discover How To Magnetically Attract
A Flood of Customers, Clients,
or Patients To Your Business

...

MAGNETIC MARKETING™ reveals a proven, more productive approach to growing any business by applying the secrets of attraction rather than pursuit. It lays out exactly how to create focused, targeted marketing that delivers the exact customers you want through a carefully engineered lead generation, conversion, and retention system.

Claim Your FREE Copy of Dan Kennedy's
MAGNETIC MARKETING™
All we ask is that you pay the shipping!

Order Your Copy at
www.MagneticMarketingBook.com